A STORY OF FAITH WHEN LIFE KEEPS COMING AT YOU

OVARIAN CANCER?

You can NOT be serious!

Janice M. Coggins, MSW

Foreword by Mike F. Janicek, M.D.

authorHOUSE®

AuthorHouse™
1663 Liberty Drive
Bloomington, IN 47403
www.authorhouse.com
Phone: 1-800-839-8640

Published by AuthorHouse 3/6/2013

ISBN: 978-1-4817-1356-6 (sc)
ISBN: 978-1-4817-1355-9 (e)

Library of Congress Control Number: 2013902350

Because of the dynamic nature of the Internet, any web addresses or links contained in this book may have changed since publication and may no longer be valid. The views expressed in this work are solely those of the author and do not necessarily reflect the views of the publisher, and the publisher hereby disclaims any responsibility for them.

Please address all inquiries to:
Janice M. Coggins
www.ovariancancerjourney.com

Editor: Barbara Crane

Cover and Interior Book Design: Fusion Creative Works,
www.fusioncw.com

First Edition

For additional copies please visit:
www.ovariancancerjourney.com

DEDICATION

*To women who are struggling with any medical adversity
and
especially in memory of women who have died
of ovarian cancer.*

*To Tom and Callie, a couple from my past, who taught me,
by example, about living in the now.*

ACKNOWLEDGMENTS

I am deeply indebted to the many people who have embraced my journey not only through cancer but through life, as well. I am especially grateful to my editor, Barbara Crane, and publisher AuthorHouse. The book really was supported by a friend, who wants to remain anonymous. Her guidance and instruction were invaluable. I would also like to thank Camille Claibourne and Skip Rendall for their contributions in the early stage of the book. Randy King, a business leader and friend, provided much needed encouragement when I was ready to give up.

My family has been an inspiration throughout the process of writing the book and LeeAnn Newcomb has offered technical, as well as emotional support. My Bible Study friends have prayed that this book becomes a reality and I am grateful for their constant support. I also acknowledge the technical support of Danielle Hatchett, Susan Miller and Laurie Ullmann. I would not have one word typed without them.

I am grateful to Dr. Mike Janicek for his dedication to women with gynecological cancers, and always a special thanks to his staff at Arizona Oncology, who are like family to me.

CONTENTS

Today may there be peace within.
May you trust that you are exactly where
you are meant to be.
May you not forget the infinite possibilities that
are born of faith, in yourself and others.
May you use the gifts that you have
received and pass on the love that has been given to you.
May you be content with yourself just the way you are.
Let this knowledge settle into your bones and allow
your soul the freedom to sing, dance, praise and love.
It is there for each and every one of us.

Mother Teresa

FOREWORD

OVARIAN CANCER:
What It Is and Why It's So Deadly

For those of you who aren't really sure what ovarian cancer is, let me tell you a few tidbits about this tenacious foe. I'll spare you rehashing the statistics. Statistics don't really help you understand why this is such a deadly disease. They just restate the painfully obvious year after year.

First, the typical ovarian cancer *isn't even really an ovarian cancer!* It is now thought that this disease originates from the fimbria—or fingers—at the end of the fallopian tube that collects the egg after ovulation. Studies have shown that the very beginnings of "ovarian cancer" can be detected microscopically in the fallopian tubes and nowhere else, and that the early cancer cells "sprinkle" themselves on the ovaries and spread throughout the peritoneal cavity without necessarily forming a visible growth on the tube itself. Thus, by this definition, ovarian cancer is inherently already a metastatic disease from day one.

This also explains why there is a disease called "primary peritoneal cancer" which is identical to ovarian cancer, and can arise even when a woman has had her ovaries removed! Doctors have known that fallopian tube cancer, ovarian cancer, and primary peritoneal cancer are essentially identical disease processes with different names, but with the same treatments and prognosis. We now finally understand *why.* And this is the *key* to understanding the disappointing progress to date in the early detection and treatment of ovarian cancer. *Know thy enemy,* if you want to understand this disease and what those experiencing it are truly facing.

If a cancer passes quickly through its pre-cancerous state undetected, and becomes metastatic the moment it is born, what hope is there for catching it before it becomes cancer? *Slim to none.* This explains why over 75% of ovarian cancers are found in the late Stages III and IV.

I have many intellectual and personal disagreements with those who vigorously promote "symptom awareness" for ovarian cancer. By the time a woman has bloating and "difficulty eating or feeling full quickly," it's already Stage III or IV. These symptoms arise from cancer cells that have spread into the upper abdomen, causing fluid to accumulate. Those with ovarian cancer who report "pelvic pressure" and "urinary symptoms" may have a large mass in the pelvis, perhaps early Stage I or II. However, it is now also thought that the less common ovarian cancers which do not spread and do not cause the upper abdominal symptoms may originate from a different mechanism, a small cystic invaginations of the ovarian outer skin that then form large relatively self-contained tumor sacs. Thus, symptom awareness may just be another way of differentiating the two basic types of ovarian cancer: misleadingly termed *early* and *late* stages, and have nothing to do with early detection.

What gets me into a disagreement with the "symptom awareness folks" is not their passionately good intentions, but the fact that even ultrasounds and CA-125 and other blood tests simply aren't effective screening tools. I hate to see a woman blame herself, or her other doctors, for not "picking up on this sooner." The "Retrospect-scope" *always* sees clearly. Most brain cancers are preceded by headaches. But urging everyone with headaches to think "brain cancer" isn't likely to effectively impact early detection of brain cancer. On the other hand, awareness of stroke symptoms, and early intervention *is* an example of important symptom awareness, because immediate intervention impacts outcomes very dramatically.

OK, so to this point we know that the typical ovarian cancer isn't even ovarian cancer, it metastasizes from the get-go, it doesn't give off symptoms before it's too late,

INTRODUCTION

THIS IS THE NOW. I am still here. Call me blessed. Call me determined. And yes, call me very grateful. Now call me a writer—because I need to share my story.

I have been diagnosed with the fifth most common cancer killer of women: ovarian cancer. I have broken through to a brighter time. My mission now is to increase the likelihood that many more stricken-women, may also live beyond the onset, diagnosis, and treatment of ovarian cancer.

This book begins with my story of being here as a survivor. I love to meet other survivors because they are like instant family. I often hug them simply because we have walked the same path.

For me, having cancer is real, and I embrace it as being part of who I am now. Just as I believe that each time Moses spoke of God, and Paul spoke of Jesus, it deepened their relationships with God. So it is with me. Telling my story often helps keep me in touch with my true self and with my God. Cancer may be part of me, but I am more than just cancer. And I refuse to give it more power than it is due.

Those of us with cancer know that everything in the world is not centered around us and our "let me tell you about my cancer" moments. We all have our days "in the ditch," as my friend Annette says—but we can't live there. It's not healthy for us. And most of us realize—that even with cancer—there are bigger global issues to address. We know, for example, that every seven seconds a third-world child dies of starvation. We understand that each year it would cost only $60 million to provide safe drinking water throughout Africa, and yet Americans spend that much on ice cream. For me, global facts like these help put my cancer in perspective.

In this book, are my thoughts, feelings, experiences, and observations. By sharing with other women what I have learned, I hope to increase the knowledge base for those who may receive this diagnosis and also help prepare the patients and their families for the struggle. It is my hope, too, that my story will lead to more of a personal involvement for the reader, thus leading to an expansion of research into ovarian cancer.

I am a passionate activist for ovarian cancer because I would like to keep any woman—even just *one*—from having to go through ovarian cancer treatment. But if you are reading this book and you currently have ovarian cancer, HOPE is all around you in survivors like me.

Talking to survivors is the best networking around. If this book helps connect you to someone you can talk to, *that* would make me happy. If, together, we can expand our preventative efforts against this disease, *that* would make me ecstatic. Because together, we can help make a difference on ovarian cancer's "front end"— awareness, early detection and research funding.

From this book, take what may be of use to you. Spread the word. Help where you can. And go with my kindest wishes and blessings.

Janice Coggins, Cancer Survivor

My help comes from the Lord, who made Heaven and Earth.
—Psalm 121: 2—

CHAPTER 1

TREKKING TO PARTS UNKNOWN

I had planned a trek in the Alps for my sixtieth birthday (2011). I booked the trip with friends and family on April 1, 2010. I was diagnosed with ovarian cancer on April 22nd. I had already sent half the cost of the trip reservation, and now my future wasn't looking very "treklike." But I did not want to cancel.

I had a year.

And I had faith.

THE FIRST SIGNS

There are not many books written specifically about ovarian cancer survivors. We are a small number compared to women with breast cancer. Never in my wildest dreams did I think I would have ovarian cancer. There is no history of it in my family. I exercised and ate a balanced diet. I was a healthy fifty-eight-year-old, in good shape. And then...

...I started having chronic back pain.

At first, I thought I had just lifted something too heavy at work. But when the pain persisted, I visited the physical therapy clinic, and they suggested traction sessions. Initially, that seemed to help, and I continued with the therapy for several sessions. But—since I had also been experiencing frequent urination (up to five times in a night)—I also made an appointment with my family physician. Ultimately, my doctor gave me a shot for the back pain. But, other than leaving a nice indentation in my buttock, it didn't help. And I'm not sure we did anything at all about the frequent urination.

At the time, I was being treated for one other persistent problem, which I now know, could have been a red flag for ovarian cancer. Bowel changes had precipitated a colonoscopy-biopsy…although I'm probably not doing it justice by calling them "changes." I went from having normal bowel movements a day to, "Let's see how many bowel movements I can have in one morning."

As these physical changes were happening, I was also trying to work at a job where a "happy face" was the most important thing you could wear to work. An irritable bowel, back pain, and "a happy face," can be mutually exclusive. But I was giving it my best shot at being a happy camper.

The final diagnosis from the colonoscopy was a condition called collagenous colitis. The advice was, *live with*

your back pain, keep exercising, and try to get some sleep.
Good luck with all that. Who would have known I had a
monstrous tumor growing inside of me that would eventually change my life?

After the Christmas holidays of 2009—five months
before I was diagnosed with ovarian cancer—I started
bleeding vaginally. After it persisted for two weeks, I
called my family physician, who got me in right away
for a trans-vaginal ultrasound. The test seemed scary, and
it took time to complete. I had a lot of fear and anxiety
about the bleeding. Many thoughts entered my mind.
Looking back, it now seems unusual that even this red
flag symptom did not get connected to a possible ovarian
cancer diagnosis.

More bad luck ensued. The ultrasound result was either read incorrectly, or it was not mine. When it got
in the hands of my family physician, it showed that I
had fibroid tumors. It also gave the dimensions of my
uterus and ovaries, which, by this time, we know had
been eclipsed by a large cancerous mass. But, going on
the results of the mistaken report, my doctor referred me
to an "outstanding" gynecologic surgeon.

I waited six weeks to be seen by this "outstanding"
surgeon. But when I finally saw her, it was not a good
experience. If I had to comment on her outward appear-
ance, I would say she'd had a very "large" weekend.

I was her first appointment on a Monday morning. I wasn't greeted…instead, I had to extend my hand. She kept her head down as she asked me "what was going on." When I said I had an onset of vaginal bleeding, she immediately responded, "I see that all the time, *nothing to worry about.*" We then moved to the exam room where she tried, unsuccessfully, to do a biopsy. Finally, giving up, she said she would "quit torturing me" until I was under anesthesia.

Had I gone through with the ablation as she planned, I might not be here today. The mass that I had was a "bleeder" as identified later in surgery. This doctor was so flippant about what she *thought* I had, that the results of continued treatment with her could have been devastating. Lucky for me, it took several weeks for them to schedule the ablation. And I took the opportunity to go shopping for another doctor.

Thank goodness for Dr. Julie Ann Heathcott of *Arizona Women's Care.* She was not only professional, she was personable. She greeted me, explained to me what she thought was going on, and definitely thought that I was in need of a hysterectomy. Fortunately, her first step was a biopsy and *not* an ablation. By now though, two more months had passed. My biopsy/ hysterectomy with Dr. Heathcott was scheduled for April 22, 2010. That was the day my life would change.

At this point, I would like to say that overall, I have had very good doctors. For the most part, I do not have hard feelings toward any specific doctor or institution. Even now, I am especially close to my family physician. When she found out I had been diagnosed with ovarian cancer, she went through my chart, page-by-page, to see what she may have missed. Throughout my chemotherapy, she called constantly to check on my progress. And, when she wasn't calling herself, she would have her assistant call. I was also assured by my gynecologist that she would follow up with the radiologist who had sent the bad report. It was very frustrating for her not to have had an accurate ultrasound, which she needed to practice good medicine.

Whoever said, "Hindsight is 20/20," was correct, and I believe…brilliant. In retrospect, I had *at least three* of the symptoms of ovarian cancer. But—when viewed as individual symptoms—they were vague. The origin for them could have been *anything*…including cancer.

Also, in hindsight, given my medical history, perhaps there could have been an additional test recommended at that time. My history included hormone replacement therapy for several years. And I do not have children. Both of those situations can increase the risk factors for ovarian cancer.

So, would it have been nice if we could have found the cancer earlier? Yes. But, we didn't. And holding anyone "hostage" for what went wrong doesn't serve me well in the long run. My focus is not in finding fault in yesterday, but finding good in today…in this moment, in this breath. I need to give my body every chance to heal, which means placing forgiveness upfront and putting distance from negative energy.

> *Be strong and take heart,*
> *All who hope in the Lord.*
> —Psalm 31:24—

One of my main reasons for writing the book is to help other women better recognize any symptoms they may be having that might be pointing to ovarian cancer. If anything strange is going on, "persist, insist, and don't resist" until you are satisfied with the answers from the medical community.

For those of you facing cancer or who have a loved one with cancer symptoms—use your voice to ask questions. And do *not* stop until you get answers. If the first doctor that you go to is the wrong fit, keep looking. Had I stayed with the first gynecologic surgeon I was referred to, I don't think my outcome would have been the same.

In the search for answers, you have to have all your senses and antennas out working for you. Women have good non-verbal communication skills. We tend to pick up on the least little bit of information coming in to us. In her book, *My Stroke of Insight,* Dr. Jill Bolt Taylor has written that we are all part of an energy field. And being *aware of that* is important.

We are consciously—and sometimes subconsciously—aware of how things feel. You have to have a good connection with your doctor and your medical community as a whole. Even if you are just going for a mammogram or blood work, make sure you are comfortable with the facility.

PAY ATTENTION and LISTEN TO YOUR INNER VOICE. Any out-of-the-ordinary symptoms that persist for over three weeks, *should be investigated.* I had my three symptoms for *a year.* And from what I have learned, it is a miracle that I am alive to tell my story.

I am grateful.

SURGERY DAY: APRIL 22, 2010

What I thought would be a routine hysterectomy based on the ultrasound, turned out to be an open and closed case. Dr. Heathcott found a large malignant mass that was bleeding. And the biopsies were positive for cancer. She immediately consulted a gynecologic oncologist/surgeon, Dr. Mike Janicek. His direction was to have Dr. Heathcott stop the bleeding and close the current procedure. After that, the plan was for Dr. Janicek to evaluate the next steps in my treatment.

I, of course, did not know the results of that surgery until much later. It was four o'clock in the morning when my friend LeeAnn came gently to my bedside and told me that I had not had a hysterectomy. And as I looked down at my sore, bandaged stomach, I said, "Well if I didn't have a hysterectomy, what did I have done?"

She did not use the "c" word. I later found out that she was told to *not* use the word *cancer.* Instead, she said, "You were opened, but they had to close you because they found *abnormal cells.*" As a social worker, having been in healthcare and having worked with hospice and cancer patients, I understood *abnormal cells,* and what that potentially meant. But I did not want to visit it at that point in time, so I just lay in my bed and closed my eyes.

We were visited by Dr. Heathcott later that morning. Although she was not on call that weekend, she made a point to see me. At that point, we did use the "c" word. She told me that she had ordered a CT scan. It was still difficult to get my head around everything. But there was so much to process, it seemed as though my psyche was shutting down.

It was extremely helpful that my nephew John and niece Callie had flown in from Mississippi and Tennessee to be with me. John and Callie are like the son and daughter that I didn't have, and my sister has been sweet enough to loan them to me throughout my life. John stayed with me the entire first week so he could be with me to meet the oncologist and hear the diagnosis.

While it was a most comforting sight to see them both in my room that morning, I also knew that, for them to be there, things must not be so good for "the ole auntie."

The CT scan was scheduled two days post-op. The attendants came to pick me up on a gurney. My family was at lunch, so I went to the CT alone. I say this for the purpose of preparing yourself for these scary moments. I knew I had cancer, but I did not know the extent or progression of the disease. I was in a hallway on a stretcher for twenty minutes awaiting the CT, and my brain was spinning in every direction. I was frightened and lonely and cold in that hallway. Had I known how frightened I would be, I would have wanted a family member with me.

When one is diagnosed with cancer there is "cause for pause." It is the one-two punch that you've always heard about. You say over and over to yourself this can*not* be happening. But, of course, it *is.*

I don't think there is any "right way" to handle the initial words when you learn you have cancer. We are all different. And we all handle it our own way and time. I am an *action* person, and I wanted to start fighting right away. So, upon my surgery discharge, Dr. Heathcott was

with a passion, listening to the same dismal picture of what could be my future. That is where the *danger* lies. So, I choose to look at what the *opportunities* are…here and NOW. What I can do NOW to be well? What can I do NOW to embrace life?

Living in the moment and being faith-based are the anchors for me. But I could not journey with cancer alone. I have my family and friends. I think it's crucial to allow yourself the grieving space you need, because it will be necessary. There are days when I'm sad. And sometimes I just need to cry. I don't like it that I have cancer. But I don't let it take my zeal for life. I wear both teal *and* zeal. (Teal is the ribbon color for ovarian cancer.)

I believe in both the power of prayer and in connecting with others. Those are serious cancer fighting tools for me. Another tool is my commitment to exercise. I especially love hiking. Being in God's playground is *so* important to me. After my treatment, I couldn't wait until I was healthy enough to get back to my physical regimen. It does take a while, though. You have to be kind to yourself and understand that your body has been through an ordeal. You can't push too much, too soon.

I'm not denying that I have cancer. And it's serious. But I have life. And it's precious.

Today I have given you the choice between life and death,
between blessings and curses.
Now I call on heaven and earth to witness the
choice you make. Oh, that you would choose life.
—Deuteronomy 30:19—

The above verse sums it up for those of us who choose to truly *live* with ovarian cancer. I believe that, in choosing to live *with* cancer, you make a *conscious* choice to do your part toward healing and health.

One of the most important things you can do is to bring your *best energy* with you when you have surgery, chemotherapy, radiation, or other treatment options. Good energy to me is having a mindset of a positive outcome to treatment. You must also bring that same good energy when you interact with the medical and support care team. A friend of mine, Randy King, states, you either deal or you're dealt. I like to think that I'm not allowing cancer to deal me *anything*.

People talk about what a major impact it is to hear the words, "You have cancer." Hearing those words from Dr. Janicek, and seeing the tumor on that screen, rocked my world. I finally understood what I was dealing with. And when Dr. Janicek laid out the treatment options, I am here to say, the fighter in me stepped up to the plate.

The treatment plan was to shrink the tumor through chemotherapy for nine weeks, and then have the debulking surgery (which included a total hysterectomy) to complete the cancer removal. After healing from *that* surgery, I would have an *additional* nine weeks of chemotherapy to remove any microscopic cancer cells that may have been left behind.

At this point, I was only five days post-op. And looking into my future, this treatment was not going to be a picnic. But, if I was going to survive, I knew I would have to put everything I had into beating this head-on. I chose to receive chemotherapy once a week (instead of once every three weeks), and I wanted to start as soon as possible. So, when Dr. Janicek asked me when I thought I could start, I said, "Whenever you clear me."

A few days later, I had a port (catheter) implanted in my upper chest to prepare for the chemotherapy. As my Mother would say, I wasn't letting any grass grow under my feet. I knew that cancer had been with me for a while, and it was time to take the reins and give it my best fight.

Two weeks after my first surgery, I began my chemotherapy. I was still too weak to open the front door of the doctor's office. But I followed whatever they told me to do to a T. I didn't dwell on the fact that I had cancer. Cancer did not define me. And it was my decision to wear a smile to chemotherapy each week.

Thich Nhat Hanh, a renowned Zen monk, suggests reciting the following lines as we breathe in and out: "Breathing in, I calm my body, breathing out, I smile. Dwelling in the present moment I know this is a wonderful moment."

My smile was about my inner joy. Not that I was joyous over having cancer—far from it. But I had a *choice* over what emotion I would carry into the chemo room. And I always chose joy.

I believed it was my way of cooperating with my treatment and the staff. The staff had their job to do. And I had mine. There is a difference between *reacting* to treatment and *responding* to treatment. I was going to do my part to *respond*. Joy can be infectious. I like to spell enjoy, "injoy," because one's joy really comes from *within*. And it can truly spread to others.

PUTTING TOGETHER MY "J" TEAM

From the minute I found out my course of treatment, I knew I had to make a plan for myself, so I began putting together a team of people—my "J" or "Jan" team who could help me in my battle. In addition to my family and friends, the people I chose were experts in their individual fields, and included a nutritionist, a physical therapist, an acupuncturist, a yoga instructor, and a spiritual director.

made a connection with all of them, and always looked forward to seeing them.

Geography, finances, an unsupportive family—any of these may make it difficult to assemble a "J" team of your own. Here are some things you can do. Do you want more information about your diagnosis? You can find it on the Internet. By the way, most public libraries have computers that will give you free Internet access and librarians who will help you learn how to use it. In addition, many chemotherapy rooms or facilities stock information for you to use.

Do you want a "buddy" to sit with you during chemotherapy? Ask the nurse if the hospital/facility has a volunteer program. One of these kind volunteers will keep your spirits up during your chemo.

THE FIRST DAYS OF CHEMO

I was first introduced to the chemo room by Kelly, the nurse practitioner at Dr Janicek's office. As Kelly told me about my new regimen, she was very thorough and professional. I, on the other hand, was numb. Although Dr. Janicek had been clear in his explanation of my situation, I was still, at times, in a state of disbelief. When Kelly told me that one of the drugs would cause me to lose my hair, I remember thinking, "Oh…you don't know me very well. That's *not* going to happen to me. I'll definitely be keeping my hair." It's clear I was still in "shock mode." Three weeks later, I was bald as a cue ball. Kelly and I still laugh about that.

The two chemotherapy drugs selected for my diagnosis were Taxol and Carboplatin. Both of these drugs were intense, and each would create a new set of challenges to live with.

When my chemo nurse Vicki called me to set up my first chemotherapy time, I was two weeks post-surgery. I really don't remember much about my first chemo day, other than being weak as a kitten.

The chemo room was a rectangular room with lounge recliners on both sides. The room could accommodate eight to ten patients. There was a small office next to the chemo room, where the nurses mixed the medications, did their charts, and made phone calls. At the opposite end of the room, was an area for us to get drinks or snacks. The room was very "home-like," making it inviting for all who entered. And it was easy to strike-up conversations with others in the room.

When friends drove me to chemo, they would bring things to do. But most of the time they became engrossed in the conversations of the chemo patients. And, over time, there were many friendships made in that space. For the chemo patients, it was the camaraderie that made the treatments palatable.

From the beginning, my chemo regimen seemed to work for me. I tolerated the chemo relatively well. There were bouts of constipation and diarrhea, which were not fun side-effects. Most of the time, they could be treated with over-the-counter medications. But occasionally, prescription medications were required.

In addition to the Taxol and Carboplatin, I also received steroids, antihistamines, and anti-nausea medication. It could be overwhelming. The steroids made me so "wired" that sleep became difficult, if not impossible. I can truthfully say that when the chemo regimen included steroids, I never slept that night. Instead, I prayed, had quiet times, and read. (Sometimes, I read the same paragraph 100 times!)

At first, I dreaded the effect of the steroids. But then, just like the cancer diagnosis, I began to embrace it for what it was, and I learned how to live on steroids. *Thank goodness* it was just for one night a week. But, after the first few times, "steroid nights" became a sacred time for me. By sacred time, I mean I prayed…and prayed…and prayed.

I now have a tip for anyone who stays up all night praying for others. I started with the first letter of the alphabet, and prayed for anyone I knew with a name starting with "A." After that, I just continued through "Z". In the same alphabetical way, I sometimes prayed for entire *countries*. In that way, I felt like I was praying for the whole world. I have to be honest, though; I am not much of a geography buff, so I could not remember *all* the countries. But, *if* it was a country and I *remembered* it, I *prayed* for it. The goal was for me to get outside myself and—rather than focus on my cancer—pray for others. Certainly, I prayed for myself, too. But I never let that be my only focus.

THE "BALD" CONNECTION

The day I got my head shaved was not as traumatic as the days leading up to it. When you begin to lose so much hair that your sink is no longer white because it's full of your hair, you know it's time to shave your head. That was the day I had my meltdown. It was brief. But, nonetheless, it was another touchstone of reality for me that this was *real*, and I was dealing with something that had my attention. I was glad I was alone that day. I could just cry and release the emotions attached to my hair, looks, or whatever else was going on. You realize you're losing ground, and you will not be your same self. It's one of those strength/surrender times I describe throughout the book. I often found myself in this same juxtaposition, having to be strong, yet really what I needed was to just surrender to the moment.

I did get through the head-shaving event. I am very fortunate that I have a friend who is a retired hairdresser.

And I believe that, through the way I became comfortable in my own skin and embraced my cancer, I was able to help other cancer patients along their journey as well. And isn't that what we're all here to do anyway? Hair or no hair.

And after all:

> *...underneath our hair we are all bald.*
> —Author Unknown—

When you don't have any hair on your head or eyebrows or eyelashes, your smile can save you. I found my smile was both internal and external. I'm not one who can fake a smile. If you can get comfortable in your own skin and allow yourself joy, it can become a tool in your arsenal. Going through cancer is tough enough. But one of the antidotes for me was just smiling. It was another part of my *"I may have cancer but it doesn't have me"* mind-set. Now that's an attitude of fortitude.

LIVING STRONG

After nine long weeks of chemo, on July 12th, my surgery date finally arrived. I was very anxious to get the cancer removed. The nurse in charge of prepping me for the surgery was starting my IV, when he looked down at my Livestrong bracelet. He asked me to take it off. When I grimaced, he asked if it was important to me. I answered, "Yes, it's very important to me. I've had it on since I was diagnosed April 22nd. It's my message to myself everyday that I have to live strong. He said, "I'm going to let you keep it on." I wore my Livestrong bracelet through my surgery. *Nothing on but my Livestrong ...so to speak.*

The Livestrong bracelets were designed by Nike, and were introduced in May 2004 to raise money for the Lance Armstrong Foundation. There have been over 70 million sold and over $325 million contributed to cancer research and education/services for survivors.

When I was first diagnosed, I knew I had to live strong physically, spiritually, and emotionally in every aspect of my life. I starting wearing my Livestrong bracelet, because whenever my family asked, "What can we do?" I always answered, "Be strong." I was going *to live strong,* and if they wanted to participate in that with me, they could wear the bracelets, too. It was special that my sister in Denver would look at her bracelet everyday and send me the message, *Live strong, Jan.*

It really is a heart-to-heart connection that I hope everybody wearing the bracelet for me has. Collectively, it has a great impact. In the mail one day, I received a picture taken on the beach. It was from my family...twenty members, all wearing their live strong bracelets, FOR ME. That picture has a prominent place in the house.

Another cool bracelet was given to me by my sister, Jeanette. It was a $4.98 bracelet she got at a Kroger grocery store in Columbus, MS. It is a stretchy bracelet, and on one side it says, *Have Faith,* and on the other side, *Expect Miracles.* That bracelet, along with my Livestrong, have been reminders of the importance of faith and family.

I also wear a to-soldier-from-soldier bracelet that my chemo friend Beth gave me. It represents the "foxhole" metaphor of being in the cancer battle together. Beth and I know what it's like to be in a fight for our lives, and we're going to be here for each other for as long as it takes. This bracelet is made by our U.S. Soldiers. Buying one of these bracelets is also a way to support our troops. Sometimes all it takes are little things to keep you stoked, focused, and grounded. Whatever it takes for you to do personally, do it.

Having a cancer diagnosis has slowed me down. I had to remove my watch to wear my bracelets. That's OK, because time just doesn't seem to have the same meaning. I don't have the same need for time as I did before. I'm not as hurried or rushed.

Do whatever you need to make yourself feel comfortable. It might not be a bracelet, it may be a special piece of jewelry, or a prayer token. Make anything that is special and meaningful to you a part of your journey.

RED BIRD

Even though the nine weeks of chemo seemed long sometimes, it was still hard to believe that my surgery on July 12th had arrived so fast. Ideally, the debulking surgery I was scheduled to have involves removing all visible cancer. The desired outcome is to have only microscopic cancer cells left, which will hopefully be killed with post-surgical chemotherapy.

My niece, Callie, and nephew, John, had flown in again to be with LeeAnn and me. On the day of the surgery, we tried to keep things as normal and calm as we could. Although I was unable to eat anything because of the surgery prep, I went to the kitchen to sit with them while they ate. Little did I know, there would be a surprise waiting for me. They were all wearing "Janice Coggins Day" T-shirts. And they weren't the *only* ones. Because, what I *also* didn't know was that weeks prior to surgery—thanks to an idea from LeeAnn and Camille—my friends and family had had pictures made wearing the same T-shirts so that they could send them to me on surgery day. The T-shirts were white with navy blue printed letters saying: *Janice Coggins Day* and a Volkswagen van picture (my favorite car). The pictures flooded my email and brightened my day. They let me know how many people were dedicating their thoughts and prayers to me on the day of my surgery.

I sat with everyone as they ate breakfast and smiled at those awesome T-shirts. Then, after they finished, we all sat by the window to have devotional. LeeAnn and I do devotionals each morning. But normally we aren't in the part of the house where we can see the back yard. On this day though, when we started the devotional, we saw a red bird—a cardinal—looking in at us from about ten feet away.

To understand the meaning of this for me, I should explain that my dad died on March 31, 2009. My dad and I were close, as are many fathers and daughters. And when he died, my mother had made arrangements for his funeral service with her two ministers, who hadn't really known him. My dad had been in a nursing home for the eight years prior to his death, with Alzheimer's disease. So the decision, that ministers who hadn't known him would be the only ones to speak at his funeral, didn't sit well with me. I called my siblings to ask if they would be okay if I said a few words at the service. They gave their permission. But, because our mother had already had everything planned, I told them I needed to pray about it.

On the morning of the service, I was outside on my mother's patio trying to get an answer as to whether I should speak, knowing that she might not approve. The next thing I knew I was visited by the most beautiful red bird I'd ever seen…and it began to sing. I smiled and

thanked God, because I had my answer. I got a [...]
a piece of paper, and I wrote about what kind of [...]
our father was. I'm glad I did. The ministers did a [...]
job, but they had not known my father as I had. I rea[...]
think that if you are going to celebrate someone's life[...]
you should consider sharing personal memories.

A few days after the service, we visited the cemetery.
I opened the car door. And, at a distance I could hear a
red bird singing. Then a moment later, he flew right by
us. And I can promise you, I let the tears wash over me,
joyful tears for my father. My father is in heaven, that
I know. And there is something real about the red bird
connection…that I know, too. That just *is*. So when the
red bird visited me on the surgery day, I knew it was a
sign that all would be just fine. And sure enough, it was.
The red bird connection is what my friend Tucker and
I call a "God shot." And I am grateful every time I see
one.

Your Father knows the things you need before you ask Him.
—Matthew 6:8—

SURGERY AND BEYOND

I am happy to say that my surgery was a success.
Dr. Janicek was able to remove the tumor and all sur-
rounding cancerous tissue. It was an extensive surgery,
and there had been some complications. But I made it

...prayers. And, after five days in ...be discharged on time. I was ...weak and strong, tired and ... peace. Now my job was to re-...gery and get ready for nine more weeks ...erapy. I was telling people that I still had the ...nine to play (using the metaphor of golf).

It seemed like an overwhelming task. *But I* am glad to be able to say that the next two-and-a-half months of treatment went off smoothly and I continued to get the same love and support from my friends, family, and the amazing "J" Team. I left chemo weak and in bad physical shape.

While chemo destroys cancer cells, it destroys healthy cells as well. And although I was beyond grateful that the chemo had saved my life, I was more than happy to now have it in my rearview mirror. Now my thoughts could *finally* turn to my future again. And there were some exciting prospects lying ahead of me. In addition to our trip to the Alps, during chemo I'd also gotten an amazing opportunity to book a trip to the Holy Land. And though my body was tired, it was crazy how quickly my mind started looking forward to our upcoming travels.

THE ALPS—ONWARD AND UPWARD (AND SOMETIMES SIDEWAYS)

Two surgeries and eighteen weeks after my diagnosis, mentally I was more than ready to hike the Alps.

Physically, though, they seemed almost insurmountable. Chemotherapy had not only left my body weak, but it had left me with serious neuropathy in my feet which affected my balance. Not exactly ideal circumstances for any hike…let alone…*The Alps*.

It is not unusual for cancer patients to have blood transfusions after extended chemotherapy regimens. Just walking a hundred yards can leave you totally exhausted. And—since it's important that you don't over exert yourself after your body has been in its lowest physical condition—I couldn't start training for two months post-chemo. But ultimately, my physical therapist, Bonnie, played an essential role in getting me in shape for the trek. I trained for the trek by actually hiking at elevation and with weight in my pack. It wasn't easy, my balance was an issue due to neuropathy. Trekking poles are essential but I still would fall.

Though I knew I would be the weakest member of the team physically, I was determined to make this trip. The only way I *wasn't* going to make it was if I died on the mountain. And, trust me, I did not pack funeral clothes for the trip. I was *going* to make it.

On July 18, 2011, I began my trek up the mountain. I was hiking the Chamonix to Zermatt Haute Route, ten months post-chemo. I was nauseated within the first hour of each hard day. And, while I wanted to blame it on the altitude, our guide, Hilary Sharp, quickly told me it was fatigue. She was right, of course. But I wasn't giving up. As I walked, I dedicated the trek to every person who had died from cancer, as well as, to every cancer *survivor*.

As I hiked, I stayed in the NOW. I had to be *present*. Every time I took a step, it was important where I placed each foot. Otherwise, I could be meeting my creator sooner than perhaps planned…and I'm not exaggerating. It was difficult. I cried every day. But I was never crying because I wanted to give up. I was crying because it was *so hard*. And cancer had been so *hard*. But when things are hard, you have to push…and then push some more. We have strength that we don't know we have.

I fell many times on the trail. One time, it was an all out face-first hard fall. At that point in the trek, the guide didn't know I had been taking cancer treatments, and she was less than compassionate. "Get up," she told me. *I just stared at her.* Of *course,* I was going to get up. But the fall had rocked me a bit. We were on snow and ice at that time…and I was carrying a heavy pack. So it was a bit more challenging for me than to simply, "get up." Even so, it ended up turning into a positive moment for me. After we were down the trail a bit, I remember thinking, "Okay, *that* was a knockdown punch. But I did it. *I got up.*"

Initially, I did not share my cancer diagnosis with my guide because I was afraid she wouldn't allow me to go on the hike. Midway through the trek, she found out by chance. She got the news that a very close friend of hers had died of cancer. And I took that opportunity to tell her about my own diagnosis. She showed great compassion. But she said that, after seeing my extreme fatigue, she had already figured out something was wrong. Still, it was good to have it out in the open.

After she knew the whole story, she really looked after me and wanted me to be successful. I can still hear her saying, "Come along, Jan." To help make my trek successful, she had me walking directly behind her. Hilary is a world-class guide. And she knew how to get over even the most compromised passes.

Winston Churchill's quote, *Never give in, never, never, never, never, never...* was presented in a speech to the students at Harrows, England in 1941. The words of that speech rang loud in my ears. And during my hike in the Alps, the quote was a mantra. I heard that message so loud sometimes that I thought my eardrums would burst.

On the last day, when we got to the last mountain pass and the final ascent, Hilary stepped aside and said to me, "Lead your team to the top, Jan." I did. But it was with a few tears...not because of the *physical* demands, but because of the sheer emotional component of what we had accomplished as a group. I didn't do it alone. I may have taken each step by myself, but I knew I had many people praying...it was almost as if I was in a zone outside myself for most of the trek.

A trek like the Haute Route forces you to be very *present*. I knew in my heart the hike was for every person cancer has touched. It is hard to explain it well. But, for me, each step was defying cancer's existence, and I saw it as a temporary way for me to have a win over cancer. It's important to get those wins when you can. But it doesn't have to be a trek in Switzerland. It can be as simple as a family gathering at the beach. The point is to set a goal and go for it, as Dr. Janicek said to me "live your life." That will mean something different for each person but "living" is the important thing, making the decision to *live*.

When you have cancer you're going to get (lots of) knockdown punches. And they don't feel good. But you get up from them the same way I got up from my falls on the mountain. And I can tell you that in the end, I came off that huge mountain using my own two legs. And, God knows, it may not have been a pretty sight—and I am so grateful that we only took *still* pictures and *not* videos—but still...I got it done.

> *We will all stumble from time to time,*
> *that's why it's helpful to hold hands.*
> —Author Unknown—

CHAPTER 2

FINDING THE SURVIVOR IN ME

I was born in Macon, Mississippi on July 22, 1951 to John and Judy Coggins. There was nothing unusual about that day, except that my mother was expecting a boy, not a girl. So the names she had picked out were for the wrong gender. As it turned out, the nurse named me. This is a story I didn't particularly like, until—later in life—I found out that Janice is the female name for John. I liked that since I was particularly close to my Dad.

In today's world, I would have been labeled *developmentally delayed.* I didn't walk until I was two. And my speech was slow as well. As I grew up, I developed a seizure disorder, which first manifested itself at a Girl Scout meeting at the age of 10. I lost bladder control and consciousness that day. We lived in rural Mississippi, and some thought that I was perhaps just *excited* about something. But with the advent of MRI (Magnetic Resonance Imaging), the doctors were able to detect extra *abnormal* lesions (which I call *rocks*) in my brain that were causing my seizure disorder. The official diagnosis of "these rocks" is *neuronal migration.* The neurons migrate to areas of the brain that can then be problematic. My "extra rocks" have housed themselves in my temporal lobe, and thus, affected my speech.

At least this has been one theory along the way. I have had many brain scans since my official 1981 seizure diagnosis. My last scan was in 2009. The radiologist reading the scan asked my friend, LeeAnn, if I was functional. She answered that I was quite functional and had a Master's Degree. He was shaking his head at what he saw on the scan but he had not seen ME! A person's brain adapts, and mine undoubtedly adapted to what it didn't know it didn't have. Some may argue, me included, that the seizures I've had haven't helped my cause but for the most part, I can get from Point A to Point B.

I started stuttering at the age of eight. It wasn't easy growing up that way. I would ask God, "Why I was the only one in my class who stuttered?" But it never seemed that I got an answer. My parents did all they could at the time. They took me to a speech therapist in Columbus, Mississippi weekly. And one of the activities the therapist had me do was "talk to trees."

I grew up in a house built in 1832. It had over thirty large oak trees in the front yard. Trust me, I could talk to *trees.* It was only when I talked to *people* that the difficulty began. In school, we had to read out loud quite often. And I always thought how cruel that was. Naturally, I wasn't ever the teacher's "pick," which frustrated me. So, it was about this time, that I started to learn how to assert myself. I got teased by the other children a lot, which was not fun. But in spite of it, I learned how to become popular. That may sound like a contradiction...being a stutterer and becoming popular. But as I look back at that now, I realize that what I had done was called, *surviving*.

Years later, I eventually chose a career in social work. It is a profession where using your voice is critical. Early in my career, there was an incident that happened which set me on a course that that would change my life.

The incident happened in my office at the medical center where I was working. When the phone rang, I answered it...or rather, I *attempted* to answer it, but nothing would come out. Completely frustrated, I did something I had never done before. I stood up, took the phone, and threw it against the cement wall. I then gathered my purse, and left for the day. I was so distraught; I got in my car and drove to a mom and pop book store in Jackson, Mississippi. There were so many things going through my head. And it didn't help that the person I had hung up on was the head nephrologist, my boss.

I found a book titled *Stuttering Solved* by Martin Schwartz, Ph.D. I believe there are no "accidents." And though I had never heard of this book or this man, I bought the book, read it, and—that same afternoon—I had my roommate Nancy contact his office and make an appointment for me.

It took a few months before I could see him. His practice was in New York City. So when the appointment date came, I packed my bags and traveled to New York University Medical Center.

I spent all my savings for travel and registration. The speech therapy was a weeklong commitment, and it was a rigorous therapy. The program focused on intense speech therapy. The doctor took three clients each week. In addition to myself, there were two gentlemen in the class. And we would spend from 9 AM on Monday until 5 PM on Friday together. We shared lunch, breaks, and tears. It was difficult. Even the introductions had been painful. The other two gentlemen took at least five minutes each just to get their names out. Then, I went. And for the first time in my life I *wanted* to stutter. But, for some reason, I *didn't*. Instead, when it got to be my turn, I spoke my name fluently.

The two gentlemen wanted to kill me, I'm sure. Dr. Schwarz said to me, "So, you *don't* stutter?" I answered, "Oh…yes, sir. I *stutter*. I promise." He then began to blast me with questions, and the stuttering crept in. I couldn't have been *happier.*

It was now only two weeks before I would begin graduate school for my master's degree in social work. We were videotaped more times than I can remember. The speech therapy treatment I had turned out to be a Godsend. Dr. Schwartz taught us to elongate the first word of every sentence, and thus, open up the vocal chords. This is why singers don't stutter, he reminded us. The country singer Mel Tillis is a great singer and yet a stutterer. Dr. Schwartz also addressed my fear of answering the phone. He took us to a phone center. And we had to call all over the United States asking questions about different topics using our new technique. It was quite an intense intervention and prepared me for graduate school.

Today, I wouldn't call myself either a stutterer *or* a fluent speaker. I'm somewhere in the middle. I've spoken in front of a thousand people and received a standing ovation. I hope the ovation was from a job well done. But perhaps it was because they were glad the speech was over! Regardless, I'm comfortable and happy in my own skin now. And I couldn't say that all my life. I once allowed being a stutterer to define me. But it doesn't anymore.

LIFE IS FRAGILE

My first job as a medical social worker was at the University Medical Center in Jackson, Mississippi. The

Medical Center has a strong social services department, and I was fortunate to get the job. The department had thirty-eight social workers and six support staff. It was headed by a woman of German ancestry. Although she was barely five feet tall, she stood at least ten feet tall in my eyes. In a matter of months, she taught me everything I would learn about social work. I thought my mother was tough. But this lady was even tougher. I respected her tremendously. And I knew I was getting an education that college had not given me.

This was *real* work. These were life and death situations. I worked in the hemodialysis and kidney transplant units. And though I knew little about that particular service coming in, I was excited to be a part of the staff, and more than willing to learn. I was able to work with physicians who were known for their excellence in kidney transplants and diseases. All was good with the job except one "minor" thing...my office was next to the morgue. I was twenty-three years old, bright-eyed and ready to save the world...*not bury* it. The hospital had over seven hundred beds. And often, when I would come out my door, someone would be going into the morgue. It was always hard to see.

Working with dialysis in the early 70's was challenging, to say the least. We had to make tough decisions. Not everyone could receive the needed treatment. Often it was due to socioeconomic issues. There were people who just couldn't afford it. Until we opened satellite units throughout the state of Mississippi, Jackson was the only site offering the treatments. If patients couldn't afford the multiple trips each week for dialysis, they may not have been candidates for the program.

Early on, I was blessed to learn how fragile life can be. My tough social work director helped me through my first death as a social worker. You don't forget that. You lose a little of yourself, in a way. But I grew exponentially from that job. And I learned that I wanted to go farther in my field, so I decided to get a graduate degree in social work. It has been one of the best decisions I have ever made. Through this amazing profession, I have been able to grow and learn and stay constantly in touch with both the toughness and the fragility of life.

After graduate school, my speech improved, and I landed a good job as director of a mental health center in Cleveland, Mississippi. It was stressful, but exciting. I had gotten my Bachelor of Science degree at Delta State in Cleveland, so I felt right at home. I became active in the community and on campus.

While attending a campus function, I had my second grand mal seizure. Again, like my first seizure when I was ten years old, I lost bladder control. This time I vomited violently for several minutes. I lost consciousness.

Cleveland's hospital was small in 1978 and the electroen-cephalogram (EEG) done was read in Atlanta, Georgia. The EEG was negative. I was not treated for a seizure disorder, even though I had been symptomatic prior to this event (but didn't know it). There was a psychiatric nurse named Alice at the mental health center, and I would tell her how I was feeling. She would look at me like I was one of the psyche patients, because that's truly what it felt like. My symptoms were vague. For instance, I would be at a stop sign, wondering whether I should go right or left, which was odd because Cleveland was not a big town. And then, suddenly I would hear rhyming words in my head. Later, I would find out this pattern was very typical of temporal lobe seizures.

I didn't have another grand mal seizure until 1981. I had moved to Lafayette, Louisiana and was working as the Director of Social Work at Our Lady of Lourdes Hospital. One day, I was having symptoms. But this time they included right arm and hand tingling, and difficulty with my speech but not stuttering, more like aphasia, which accompanies a stroke. I had only been with the hospital three months, but that was long enough to make significant contacts. And one of them was a neurosurgeon who practiced at the hospital. I knew I didn't need neurosurgery, but I thought he may have some answers.

The next day, I walked into his office and asked to see him.

You *know* it is a miracle when you can walk into a M.D.'s office and get to see a doctor without an appointment. He knew I was scared. He listened to my story, gave me a quick exam, and told me I needed to see a neurologist. And he sent me to see Dr. Robert Martinez, who became my neurologist for the next twenty years. When I got my first appointment with him, everything checked out normally. But one month after my initial visit, I had another grand mal seizure. And I was taken to Our Lady of Lourdes Hospital.

During my hospitalization, Dr. Martinez came into my room and told me that they thought they had "missed something" in the EEG. Dr. Martinez ordered another EEG. But this time they used leads up the nose that rested on the temporal lobe. During the procedure, you can't move at all. Tears ran down my nose and face. But the temporal lobe was where they found my problem. The EEG tech paged Dr. Martinez while she was performing the EEG. She was so proud that she had finally solved the puzzle. When Dr. Martinez saw it, he, too, knew he had figured out what was going on with me. Later, an MRI would further validate the diagnosis of the temporal lobe irregularity.

I have been on many different seizure meds since 1981. Some require weekly blood work. And some left me feeling less than well. But fortunately, the only restrictions I currently have from the seizure disorder are that I can't swim alone or fly an airplane. I think I can live with those restrictions.

During my treatment plan, there was difficulty regulating my medications, so Dr. Martinez referred me to the Bowman Gray Medical Center in Winston-Salem, North Carolina to see Dr. J. Kiffin Penry. Dr. Penry wrote the textbook on seizures, so to speak. I spent a week with Dr. Penry and his staff and learned the importance of taking seizure meds with regularity and sleeping well.

My seizures have been harder on my caregivers than me. It's a frightening experience to come out of a seizure. I can only imagine what it's like to *watch* the process. But I am grateful I have people in my life who have helped me through those moments and who love me.

Dr. Martinez was more than just a doctor to me. He took a special interest in my case and wanted me to do well. He died a few years ago of cancer. I grieved when I learned of his death. The healthcare community lost a wonderful provider of healing care. And to this day, I still miss him terribly.

I used to be resentful that I was a stutterer and had a seizure disorder. Both are very rare. There's a low percentage of female stutterers, and there are only three million Americans with a seizure disorder. Fortunately, as we grow older, and hopefully wiser, we learn to move from resentment to contentment. Or as I now like to say, *I am comfortable in my own skin.*

Whether I stutter, have a seizure disorder, or have cancer, none of them should define who I am as a person. They are just *part* of who I am. And, for the most part, they have brought me more richness. According to my spiritual director, Sister Barb, they have also brought me *character.* I jokingly tell her, "No more character... please." But from my stuttering I learned toughness. And I also learned that I don't have to be perfect. We are all flawed in some way. My stuttering and seizures were audible and visible...and as a child, painful. But, because of them, I learned compassion at an early age. And to this day I always root for the underdog.

CHAPTER 3

SMILES AND INSPIRATION

Just as I grew through my job as a social worker, I have grown through my cancer experience. There have been so many special moments that I have gone through, both alone and with loved ones that have changed my life forever. There have been funny moments and poignant moments and desperately sad moments. And there have been many moments filled with hope and joy.

Through the people I met and the challenges I faced, I gained both perspective and balance. As I made connections with other cancer patients along the way, they told me about their own experiences. Each of our cancer journeys is unique. Each has its own message. And each is inspirational in its own way. I've put some of my favorite stories in the section below. I hope that, as you read them, some will evoke a smile or two, others will cause you to think, and perhaps some others will create an even deeper connection.

It is what it is, but it will be what we make it.
—Pat Summit, Tennessee Volunteers, Head Coach—

HEART-TO-HEART CONNECTIONS

One beautiful fall day, some friends and I were having lunch at a restaurant in Salida, Colorado on the Arkansas River. A woman came over to me and said, "I've got to comment on your boldness. I had cancer seventeen years ago, and I was never able to go bald. I had to wear a wig." She told me she was in "awe of me" because I could do this.

As she talked, she began to share more of her story. She said that she'd had breast cancer. And one day, she had been in her oncologist's office, crying. She told him that she thought she was dying. Her oncologist looked at her, and said, "Rita, you have *got* to find something *to live for* and hang on to that."

She said that she thought about that for a minute and then told him, "I have a one-year-old grandchild." "Then live for that grandchild," he said. So that is what she did. She lived for that child. And now it was seventeen years later. And she was still doing well.

We had a delightful time sharing other stories about our cancer journey, too. And when she got ready to leave the restaurant, she asked if she could give me a hug. "Absolutely," I said. And, for me, that hug was truly a heart-to-heart connection.

On the same day, while still in Salida, we went into a little gift shop called, *The Bear Necessities*. A woman promptly greeted us and offered us homemade fudge. I declined it saying, "Oh no, I better not. I have cancer. I better not feed it any more sugar than it needs." At that point, she looked back at me and said, "Oh honey, I can tell you I've beaten cancer *twice*. The first time was forty years ago, and it was *ovarian*. They did a hysterectomy and didn't give me great odds. But I looked at that doctor and I told him I had a 'scumbag' for a husband and a nine-week-old baby, and I did *not* want my husband raising my child...so I want to live!"

What a great story. She lived through that ovarian cancer. And a few years ago, she also made it through breast cancer. I have never seen a woman more full of life than this woman. "It's all about attitude," she told me. Then she looked at my bald head, and said, "I've had two sets of hair come in. And when yours comes in it will have more body. *And* will be two different colors. You'll just have *a ball* with your new hair! So there's nothing to worry about there, *either*."

What a day. I'd had two amazing encounters with two incredible women who had *each* shared their courageous journeys through cancer. I was wowed and uplifted by both of them. And—since I am convinced that there are *no accidents*—it made the day all the more amazing.

A KIND WORD

One day, post-chemo, I was at sitting at a car wash waiting for the attendants to finish my car. There was a lady sitting next to me on the bench, and we struck up a conversation. She asked me about the Keen sandals that I was wearing. We proceeded to have a conversation about how comfortable Keen's are. That led to a conversation about the outdoors and hiking. I told her that I was planning to hike the Alps for my sixtieth birthday. I also told her that I hadn't been able to train yet, because I had obviously just been though chemo. She asked me how it was going. But before we could talk about it, her car was ready, and she had to go. When she stood up, she reached over, and gave me a hug and a kiss on the side of my face. "I wish you well," she said. "You just continue to do what you're doing, and I know you are going to be just fine."

It was another heart-felt connection. In that very short amount of time, that woman filled me with joy. This is one way that we can *all* "pay it forward." It didn't cost either one of us anything to have that simple human exchange. To me, this is the essence of being human. Finding moments to share with others—even if they're strangers—is what life is all about.

A VOICE FROM THE PAST

One day, I received a phone call from a voice that I hadn't heard in thirteen years. It was a voice that I truly never thought I would hear from again. I don't mean that to be disrespectful or sacrilegious when I say this, but it was almost like getting a phone call from heaven. But the call was from the CEO of the hospital where I had worked. And he was a very *big person* in my life. He had a big voice that was unforgettable...deep, distinct, and sometimes scary.

I had a good relationship with this man at Lafayette General Medical Center, Lafayette, Louisiana. My friend, Camille, had called to tell him about my cancer diagnosis. It was a Saturday morning the day he called, and I was four weeks into my chemo. When my cell phone rang, I didn't recognize the number. But when I answered, and heard that deep voice say, "Hello, Janice. This is JJ Burdin." I literally almost dropped the phone. We probably talked twenty minutes or more about old times. And he thanked me for the contributions I'd made to the hospital. We talked about our relationship and how productive it had been...and the humor we had shared. The conversation was unbelievable and memorable. He lifted me up at a time when I so needed it.

Months following that call, he himself was diagnosed with cancer. And shockingly he died six months after we

Elvie turned out to be a *great* recruiter, but working in the hospital could be stressful. We liked to have fun at times. On one particular day I decided to give her something extra to smile about. Elvie is 5'10, slim, and attractive, with long black curly hair. I'm 5'7 with short brown curly hair (pre-chemo). Elvie had a favorite dress she would wear often. It was long and pretty, and made her look very slim. As I was shopping one day, I found the exact dress in the store. And something possessed me to buy it! I've never done anything quite like this before. But after I bought the dress, I went to a wig shop and bought a long black curly wig. The next day, I had the outfit in the car, and I waited there to see what Elvie was wearing. As I said, it *was* her favorite dress. And, as I'd hoped, she had it on.

Quickly, I put on the dress and wig. Then I went into the hospital just like I owned the place. What was I *thinking?* I really don't know. But everyone was smiling at me, and some were doing double takes. As I passed them, I told them I wanted to be like Elvie when I grew up.

Then, suddenly, there she was…Elvie, herself. She looked at me like she'd just met herself in the hallway. She couldn't contain herself…nor could I. We went everywhere together that day. We greeted nurses, patients, and visitors. Our vice-president was quite amused. From that day on, Elvie and I were "tighter than ticks" (a good old Southern saying that really gets the meaning across). Fourteen years later, when Elvie heard I had cancer, she sent me a prayer text every day. That's the kind of friend you'll wear a wig for any day.

THE NORM CHARM

I have a dear friend, Norma, who is an outpatient surgery nurse. She's told me how she makes a point to connect with her patients before they go under the anesthesia to help relieve them of any anxiety. She's emphasized how important it is for her to have eye-to-eye contact.

Norma recently related a story of an ovarian cancer patient in her forties, who was coming in for routine gall bladder surgery. Of course, as we all know, if you're the patient, there is no such thing as a *routine surgery*. And this patient was very tense. So Norma knew she not only needed eye-to-eye contact...but she needed what she calls, "The Norm Charm." *Humor.* So she told the patient, "You have nothing to worry about. We've already *practiced* this operation three times today on different people." Norma says this comment always breaks the ice and eases the anxiety, I have to say that using humor in the way Norma does is just good nursing. Good nurses know what technical skills to use, as well as, what *psychosocial* skills are needed. When you're in chemotherapy, you see your chemo nurses on a weekly basis and develop close relationships. I don't know of one cancer patient who has spoken ill of their chemo nurse. I know I would walk to the ends of the earth for mine.

PRAYER WITH CHEMO

I have a dear friend named Tucker. He is a golf professional whom I worked with in the golf shop. During my cancer treatment, Tucker brought me a St. Peregrine card and pocket rosary. St. Peregrine is the patron saint of cancer victims. I put the rosary in my pocket on chemo days. It was one of those reminders that someone who sincerely cares, gave me something special. And I enjoyed having the patron saint of cancer with me. For me, *prayer with chemo* was standard on the menu as far as I was concerned.

Tucker called me every two or three days to check in on me. He even had his mother, Jill, bring me lunch one day. Even though I had only met her once, Jill called out-of-the-blue, and said, "Hey…I'm bringing us lunch." Tucker is young enough to be my own son, and he called me his "Work Mom." So Jill and I already had a lot in common. We shared our favorite reading material that day and had a wonderful visit. I connected with her in a genuinely heartfelt way, as if we had known each other for years.

KANDY AND GINGER

Sometimes when you least expect it an angel appears. That's exactly what happened when a lady named Kandy, sent me a case of ginger chews. Though I didn't know

Kandy at all, we shared the same physical and massage therapists. And, through them, she learned of my cancer.

Ginger is excellent in helping with nausea. And I ended up sharing the ginger chews with my friends in chemo, and telling them the story about our angel, Kandy. Even though I am off chemotherapy now, Kandy still sends me cases of ginger. With this generous gift, I get to play Santa Claus and hand it out to those in need.

I was recently attending a meeting on "Spirituality and Aging", where I met a wonderful woman going through treatment for ovarian cancer. I told her about the ginger, and asked her if she'd like to have some. When she said she would, I packaged up several bags and sent them to her. I received a note from her a few days later, saying how helpful it had been and how she was sharing with others. This is just another way we can do small acts of kindness, as well as pay it forward.

SISTERS

I graduated in 1973, from a small university in rural Mississippi. I was told sororities would help keep your grades up and find boyfriends. That didn't seem like a bad deal to me, so I joined Kappa Delta. What I didn't realize is that a sorority would afford you an instant set of friends that you will have for the rest of life. When one of my sorority sisters found out I had cancer, I began getting emails from people I had not heard from since the year we had graduated.

The things that they said to me, and the prayer lists that they had me on, meant so much. There are many positive aspects to sororities and fraternities that last a lifetime. We're planning a reunion sometime in the near future, and I'm sure it will be a great celebration. One of my sorority sisters is fighting ovarian cancer like me, while another sister lost her only son, in Iraq. We'll have many reasons to laugh and to cry together. We may not have seen each other in years, but our memories serve us well. And, once committed, we will always be there for each other. Once again, I count myself fortunate.

HAPPY TRAILS

LeeAnn and I met Paul two years ago on a hiking trail in Colorado. He was in Crestone on a sabbatical from his company in Texas. He had decided to go on a spiritual retreat, and he had chosen the Nada Retreat Center in Crestone, Colorado. I think it was our dog Hudson who "encouraged" us to stop and chat with him on the trail that day. Dogs are always good conversation starters, it seems. And Hudson really seemed to like Paul. And as we chatted, he ended up sitting on Paul's feet. "I think my dog really likes you," I said. And with that,

Paul seemed to feel comfortable and started telling us his story…which included both his illness and some great Texas football stories.

It turns out that Paul had gone through major heart surgery. And, for several weeks afterward, he had been emotionally and physically down. He said he had never really appreciated the value of friendship until a friend began calling him every night at the same time for weeks. Paul told us that sometimes their conversations would be five minutes, and other times, much longer. But, the one thing he knew in his recovery, was that he could count on that phone call from his friend.

Paul told us the *other* thing that was helpful in his recovery was a new puppy his daughter had brought him. We agreed that those of us who have dogs know the value of friendship with pets.

Paul had a spark about him that was contagious. We talked to him for thirty minutes. And when LeeAnn and I left him, we talked about what a cool encounter that had been. I think Paul will continue to do well in his recovery. He was already working on his physical being by taking a beautiful hike. He was on a spiritual retreat, re-connecting with friends, and talking about his family. We loved talking to him. And it turns out that he was one heck of a football player in his day. Happy trails, Paul.

PAY IT FORWARD

REI is one of my favorite stores in the world. I love the outdoors so I guess that makes me a natural fit for all of their products. I was shopping there one day, and was in line to wait for one of the registers. There was a young man at one of the registers who wasn't wearing a name badge. I remember thinking to myself that he must be a rookie. But as the line kept inching up, it looked as if I was going to get him.

There are no accidents. I ended up at his register. And I saw he was wearing a teal bracelet. Of course, I asked him about it. And he began to tell me about his wife who had ovarian cancer. I asked him how she was doing; he told me that she had died five years ago. He said that he had a blog and raised money for awareness of ovarian cancer. He said he also rides his bike regularly in her memory. Our connection was immediate. I was wearing my teal bracelet. And I told him that his wife's story and mine were very similar. I also told him the clothes that I was purchasing were for my hike in the Alp's to celebrate my sixtieth birthday and being cancer-free. He introduced himself, and told me he was one of the store managers. After I left, I thought about him often, and I carried his encounter with me. There were times in the Alps, that I would think about the chance meeting with Brad…and how he is still so passionate about ovarian cancer. After I got back from the Alps trek, I went to his blog site and saw he had posted a note wishing me the best on my trek. Sometimes you get wonderful surprises, even if they are cancer-related. Brad is at the top of my list.

MILLIE

Sometimes it's the small things you can do for yourself that may just be the antidote you need. Since 1976, I've owned a total of four Volkswagen campers. Some were kept around longer than others. But all were well-loved. I think Volkswagen camper people all love each other as well. You'll never meet one on the road without getting a big wave and a smile. It's freakish how it's almost cult-like.

At the time I was diagnosed, I didn't have a Volkswagen Camper. I was driving a CRV Honda, which I loved. But having cancer, I have only the NOW. So I started wanting all the things that I love around me...and one of those things was a Volkswagen Camper.

I found one in Oregon. It had belonged to a retired engineer named Bob Brock. He was its only owner. And it was in perfect condition. Bob and I started emailing. And the rest is history. I named her Millie, and she's occupying the third row in the garage right now. Millie has a few miles on her. But I do, too. And we are growing old together.

I have a wonderful mechanic, Mark, that I trust implicitly, who will see Millie and me through the end. Millie has been taken good care of, she looks great...and I feel like a kid when I drive her. There are times I have to fight back the tears because of the freedom I feel when I am behind that big steering wheel.

At the time I purchased her, I was probably thinking, "Oh, my gosh! I may be dying. I better do everything I want to do now." And if that was my motivation, then good. Because as the song says, we should all *live like we were dying.*

STAGE OF LIFE

My friend Annette is President of the Ovarian Cancer Alliance of Arizona and on the national board, also. When speaking at a ladies circle about ovarian cancer, she asked each of the twenty attendees to introduce themselves and say a few words about why they were there. The introductions took an hour-and-a-half. Each woman was so wrapped up in her own ovarian cancer story, that's all we ended up knowing about them—their cancer.

The impact this story made on me was that we can ill afford to give all our energy to the disease. For me, the cancer is bad enough. The last thing I need to do is to feed it.

This is why—when someone asks me what *stage* I'm in—I'm always going to answer, "the stage of life." And, in some settings it may be healthy and necessary. Share your stories, just don't allow the cancer diagnosis to *consume* you…because, it *can*. And if you give it the energy, it *will*.

I was attending a breakfast for the Ovarian Cancer Alliance of Arizona with my friend Beth and her husband. We had driven to downtown Phoenix for a wonderful program/discussion on ovarian cancer research and future modalities. At our table was a Masters-degreed nurse, who worked in oncology. Beth and I were both still bald from chemotherapy. When we introduced ourselves before the program began, the nurse asked us what stages we were in. Beth answered, "Stage Four." When the woman turned to me with the same question, I answered, "stage of life." "That's an interesting answer," she said. I looked at her, incredulously. "It's the *only* answer," I replied. Beth later told me that she wished she had said that. I told her that from then on, she *could say that*. Whatever personal information she chose to share with strangers was *really* up to her.

The question to Beth and me about what "stage we were in" seemed to cross a line for both of us. While the nurse may have had good intentions, we were not her patients. Until that moment, I did not even know what stage Beth was in; in fact, I was uncomfortable knowing it. A better question would have been, "How are you

Breakfast was delightful. And before departing, we hugged and said, "We love you." *I love you* has become standard language with me to my friends and family now.

While driving home LeeAnn and I commented on how significant relationships have become to us since cancer. Here we had just shared breakfast with two people we didn't even know a year ago… and now we claim them as two very dear friends. The difference now, is that as a cancer survivor, I don't have the luxury to allow friendships to develop *over time*. Friendships just happen now…in a very real way, in real time, without any superficiality. Cancer survivors and their families also make time for each other because they know the *value* of time…a gift cancer has given us.

I can probably speak for many, that the friends that you connect with after cancer will be heart-felt and God-driven. It's what many of us long for. And I'm not sure why we have to have a crisis like cancer for it to happen. All I know for sure is that friendships and family relationships are now solid as rock for me. And I'm sure my friend Beth feels the same way.

CELEBRATE!

I often refer to my friend Beth as my *foxhole buddy*. When I drove twelve hours from Colorado to be with her on her last day of chemo, Dr. Janicek was in disbelief. I had to *enlighten* him that that's just what *foxhole buddies* do.

The original plan was for me to Skype Beth on her last day. But I decided that Skype wasn't going to quite get it done, and I needed to actually be there. I had learned that Beth had really been struggling towards the end of chemo. My "new plan" was to show up in person in the chemo room at the exact time I was supposed to Skype her. At ten o'clock in the morning, I bounced into the chemo room with a bottle of champagne, and greeting card loudly playing, *Celebrate! Celebrate!* And there was a *lot* of celebration going on! It was one of the coolest things I've ever done...not for myself, but to truly rejoice for someone else. I think to this day Beth and I understand what we did for each other during our months of treatment. The true gift, is the gift of yourself.

DEE'S "SENSE OF WELLNESS"

I met Dee Cupchak while she was taking yoga (and I was taking Tai Chi) at the Virginia Piper Center in Scottsdale, Arizona. Dee had been diagnosed with Stage IV ovarian cancer in 2006, and was basically not given any chance for survival. I had the privilege to interview Dee, and when I asked her what she considered to be the scariest part of her ordeal, she said it was making her funeral arrangements. But, she went on to say, at some point during her treatment, she decided that she was not ready to die.

Dee had lots of people praying for her. And she did her own interventions through meditation, prayer, and empowering her own "sense of wellness." As Dee likes to put it, she believes that we all can create our wellness. It's been five years, and she's cancer-free. Dee said that when her doctor told her she was in remission, she said, "No. I am *healed.*" And that is the way she feels.

Even though Dee was not given a lot of hope, she believes in her faith, a positive attitude, and staying active. She does not see herself as a victim. She also believes in giving thanks for the healing before you receive it. Dee believes that we all are here for a purpose. And she makes a conscious effort at being grateful and praying for others.

NEIGHBORS HELPING NEIGHBORS

After I finished chemotherapy, I was lucky enough to spend the month of October resting and recuperating in the small town of Crestone, Colorado. While there, our hot water heater went out, and a great guy named Steve came to the rescue. I had met him the year before. But this time, when I greeted him at the door, I was bald. So I told him that I had just finished chemotherapy. We chatted for a while. Then, he fixed the hot water heater, and wished me well. But later—when he called me about the bill—he told me that he had several friends who had been through chemotherapy, and he knew what a financial burden it could be. He said he was willing to take at least half off my bill. I was so taken back by that, I didn't know what to say. Finally, I told him I was fortunate enough to have good insurance that covered my treatment, and that I would like to pay the full bill. But Steve's selfless offer is still one of the most touching acts of kindness and altruism I have ever seen.

In the Crestone community, there is a group there called *Neighbors Helping Neighbors.* Shortly after I moved there, they had a benefit for a woman who had been diagnosed with colon cancer, and who had no insurance. In these tough times, it's wonderful to see people reaching out from their hearts and touching others. During my years as a social worker, I have witnessed many acts of kindness and compassion. But there is certain compassion that is associated with chemotherapy that I haven't really been witness to before. It is truly palpable.

KATHY'S QUILT

LeeAnn's friend, Kathy, had breast cancer five years ago. During my treatment, she brought me a quilt that she had quilted herself, and that she wanted me to use as my chemo blanket. (It was *always* cold in the chemo room. And I always needed a blanket.) It was such a cool quilt. One side of it was really cheery...for the "cheery days" when you were having a great day. But the other side had little squares where people were using umbrellas. So, its message was that, you could also be having a "rainy day."

I had only met Kathy a few times. But she understood the cancer journey and what it took to go through it. What a great gift. It really shows the camaraderie, and the deep sense of understanding that people going through cancer have for each other. You can look in each other's eyes, and you understand where that other person has been. And when you meet another survivor, you high-five, or you shake their hand, and congratulate them… and you mean it from the heart. It's a wonderful thing.

The quilt from Kathy is now in the room in my home that's called the sanctuary. It's my spiritual room where I do a lot of my meditation, prayer, and centering. The quilt sits at the end of the sofa. I still use it as a lap blanket. Thank you, Kathy.

I received another blanket in the mail from my friend, Nancy, in Lafayette. This one was from a blanket ministry in Lafayette. Ladies from one of the churches had specifically made the blanket. It arrived with special blessings for the sick. Both blankets got much use during my weeks of treatment, and I know they both were given to me with so much care and compassion.

IT'S YOUR ALIVE DAY!

Throughout my diagnosis and treatment, I met many cancer survivors whose stories lifted my spirits and gave me strength and joy. But cancer doesn't own the market on inspirational survivor stories, and some of my greatest sources of inspiration came from people who have survived life challenges *other* than cancer.

Brian was one of them. I was handing out symptom cards for an ovarian cancer awareness event in Tempe, Arizona, when he came by the table. He was wearing a very cool T-shirt. And I jokingly asked him if I could buy it. He laughed and said that it was his "company T-shirt." He offered to run to his near-by office and get me one. The logo on the shirt was the Hawaiian sign for "hang loose." I had to know more.

As I learned, Brian had been born with Arteriovenous Malformation in his right calf and ankle. AVM is an abnormal connection between the arteries and veins in the brain, which usually forms before birth. It affects less than 1% of the population.

Brian had been limited in what sports he could play as a child. But, as an adult, he had undergone major surgeries to help resolve the pain that is associated with this diagnosis. He told me that during one procedure, things went wrong, and he had gone into cardiac arrest. Forty-five minutes later they were able to stabilize him. Most people don't survive such an ordeal. But Brian walked out of the hospital unharmed (but not unchanged) from it…a miracle.

Before the incident, Brian had been successful in the mortgage industry. But, his near-death experience changed his outlook on life, and he began pursuing his passion: a love for water and the outdoors. He and a friend started manufacturing and distributing Shaka Boards—stand-up paddleboards. He started a company called I-YAD (It's Your Alive Day) Adventures, which offers SUP tours, along with yoga and fitness classes.

Brian and I share a similar life philosophy. I love wearing my T-shirt and knowing that Brian is loving life and making a difference.

ROSEMARY

Of all the people I've known, I owe Rosemary the greatest thanks for teaching me how to live in my own skin, whatever I'm up against.

I was blessed to meet Rosemary when I was 22 years old, living in Jackson, Mississippi. I had moved to an apartment complex next to the University Medical Center where I had taken a job as a medical social worker. After I moved in, the apartment manager called me into her office. I couldn't imagine what she needed to discuss since

I hadn't participated in any rowdy parties yet. She began telling me about a woman my age, named Rosemary, who was born without arms. Also, one of her legs was much shorter than the other. Her disability was caused by the drug Thalidomide, which was given to pregnant women in the 1950's as a sleep aid and to treat morning sickness. Her mother was one of thousands who gave birth to children with serious birth defects.

The apartment manager told me that Rosemary would need assistance getting dressed in the morning, and she asked if I would be available. We set up a time for Rosemary and me to meet. Soon, we began helping each other. I honestly think I am the one who received the most help. Rosemary impacted my life beyond my ability to even explain. But, unfortunately, I never told her what she meant to me. When I moved from Jackson to go to graduate school, I lost contact with Rosemary. It wasn't until years later that I realized how much her attitude towards her disability had really impacted me.

For Rosemary, just to open the door to her apartment took a Herculean effort. She would put her key into her mouth and then turn the knob with her chin. Rosemary could write better than I could by using her toes. And she never looked at herself as *disabled*. Rosemary often talked about dating and wanting to get married. The year

I assisted Rosemary, I never allowed myself to get depressed about my stuttering. Rosemary's joy was so infectious it made me feel ashamed of myself. If we had more Rosemary's in the world who, without complaint, took the cards they are dealt, they could show the rest of us how to play. Rosemary lived in the apartment complex because she worked at vocational rehabilitation, and she was not going to allow any boundaries to stop her. She was my example of someone living a joy FULL life. I have been a more blessed person because of having met Rosemary. I wish I had told her in person. But if she ever reads this…*thank you, Rosemary.*

FROG EYES AND CHEMO BRAIN

This story is mine and it's hardly "inspirational." But I hope it will make you laugh.

During my time in chemotherapy, I decided that I needed to do something to keep myself busy around the house. Outside, sitting on my patio furniture, I have two "metal frogs." They are really cute additions to the end tables. But, I live in Arizona. And in the intense summer heat, a couple of the frog eyes had fallen out over the years. So one day, with my chemo steroids on board, I thought I would make myself useful and put them back together.

I remember Peyton, my great nephew, telling me that "Gorilla Glue" was good for projects like this. So I purchased a tube and set out to fix the frogs. I put down newspaper all over the kitchen table, brought the frogs inside, and washed and dried their little eyes. Then, I put on the glue and attached their eyes to their sockets. I held them there for about a minute and walked away. That was the end of my project…I *thought*.

Hours later, I came back to check on them. That's when I discovered that their eyes had somehow "rearranged" themselves. Two frog eyes were staring back at me in a rather startling way. One was looking at me from the floor, and the other from the kitchen table. And *both* were attached to their new surfaces. And when I say attached, I mean *attached*.

I don't know how the eye on the table wandered off the newspaper. But, trust me, it did. I just started laughing. This was truly an "I Love Lucy" moment. I told myself it was one of those "chemo brain moments" I had been told about. At least, that's what I hoped it was. (As I have since been told, I should have *held* the eyes in the sockets much longer, but how was I supposed to know? I didn't get a degree in *glue management*.) To this day, we *still* have one frog eye attached to the glass top table. I am *not* kidding. We have tried everything under the sun to remove it from the table. But it's now become just a part of the kitchen. We call it "the chemo eye."

Sometimes I really needed breakthrough moments like this one to help me release, have fun, and laugh again. I *could* enjoy myself while fighting cancer. I *could* still laugh. Those moments are special to me. And I think we all need many more of those…and not just those of us who are going through chemo. We need more of them in life in general.

CHAPTER 4

MY JOURNEY OF FAITH AND SPIRIT

I was on a journey from sickness to healing, but I was also on a spiritual journey that was just as meaningful. For me, the road to physical healing would not have been possible without my spiritual strength, guidance, and beliefs. Being a cancer patient, and now, a survivor, has allowed me to put my thoughts and beliefs into words that give me strength each day.

I believe it is better not to focus on the fact that I have cancer but rather how I am being changed by cancer. Life is not about what we *have*. It is about who we become as human beings, and it is an ever-changing process. I am a better person since my diagnosis. I am much more patient with both myself, and others. There is not a moment that goes by that I am not grateful.

This is why the NOW is so very important. We can only control what happens to us NOW. With cancer, it's easy to get ahead of yourself and start thinking about all the blood work and tests that are due next week. But if we give in to this, we miss out on some spectacular opportunities that are happening in the NOW. Besides, NOW spelled backwards is WON...if you stay in the now, you've won the day.

Cancer survivors get a double dose of knowing how to live in the moment. Cancer survivors don't count days, they make the days count. Cancer is the big teacher, and we can become its grateful pupil by allowing grace to unfold. The center of our eyes is the pupil whereby we receive sight, the same must be true with our cancer. We must be able to see *through it* to receive its *gifts*, and not just its *pain*. One of my favorite quotes is from Abraham Lincoln: "It's not the years in your life that count; it's the life in your years." Another favorite quote reflects how I feel about my faith, both before and after my cancer: "Life is *fragile;* handle with *prayer.*"

If you allow it to happen, cancer can help give your life focus. When you get a cancer diagnosis, your life suddenly has a definition it didn't have before. Of course, we all know we are going to die one day. But when you carry a cancer diagnosis, you get reminded of that *deadline* more often than you would like.

On our infamous Alps trip, our mantra was *faith, focus and finish.* That mantra is responsible for getting us over some very steep mountain passes. However—during my cancer journey—*family, friends, faith, focus and finish* was the major mindset for me every day. These anchors are instrumental in my healing process each and every day. I hope in some way, they may speak to you. Even today, I wear custom Nike shoes with the words *focus* and *faith* written on the back of them. I like to think I still have work to do so I am not quite finished!

FAMILY

Family is very important to me. I wrote a letter to my family when I was half way through treatment to tell them how they had helped me.

August 2010

Dear Family,

I am halfway to where I want to be and I couldn't be here without you. I feel compelled to write you all a BIG thank you for getting me this far. It has been a long journey since April 22nd. Many of you have said it seems like it has flown by, and in some ways that is true. On the other hand some days it seems I am waking up from a bad dream, but nevertheless, because of you we have taken cancer by the horns and faced it head on. Nine more weeks, and we will have it in our rear view mirror. God is good. I have lived each day with a grateful heart, grateful for each of you and grateful that the cancer was contained to the pelvic wall. I have been blessed throughout this journey; each day I have received a blessing that only on this journey I would have reaped.

Each of you has played such a role in helping me be strong in the face of such a wicked disease. There is nothing fun about hearing you have a tumor and it is cancer and you need chemo, surgery, etc. I was totally healthy, so I thought; you can imagine the shock I was in for days. Again, our Lord provided the strength and courage to step into a whole new world. The chemo treatments have been manageable. Chemo is your life line; you just learn to treat the side effects. Some are more lasting, but in the scheme of things (like your life), numb, tingling feet don't really matter. You just might need to watch the side of the mountain when hiking (ha!).

Suzie, your trips out here were not only fun, you were the first in the family to see my bald head and to give me so much encouragement. John and Jeanette drove 25 hours one way to bring me homegrown vegetables and presents from their friends, shared my birthday and brought homemade fig preserves from Mama. I thought it was Christmas! All of my adult life I had had the privilege of having two children vicariously (John and Callie). Jeanette willed them to me, I think, years ago. I was blessed to have them with me for both surgeries; I can never thank them enough for how that touched my soul. Matt and Leah's picture standing by the "Never Quit" statue at Ole Miss was the coolest, and of course they looked adorable in their "Janice Coggins Day" T-shirts. Kelsey calling all the way from South Africa. Who can top that? Lauren has kept her ole Auntie in the loop with beautiful pics that make us smile. Recently, I received an e-mail from a friend of hers in Roanoke, VA that started "Dear Aunt Janice, I am praying for you. "Tearfully, I thanked God again for my family. I know my Mother never goes to bed without praying for me. I must mention that her Sunday school class has sent me numerous cards as well as Jeanette's church. All of these things have sustained me throughout this journey, greater than any physical food that one could ingest.

Your prayers, which I know have been constant, are such a comfort. I would get your texts, e-mails, cards, gifts, etc., and they would come at the ideal time. To be perfectly honest, I was frightened about the July 12 surgery because I had learned that the tumor I had was a bleeder (from the surgery in April). I don't have a strong blood pressure as it is, so I was a bit nervous, but again our God is so good. LeeAnn and I had two angels out here with us before that surgery: John and Callie. The morning of my surgery we had devotional here at the house and the red bird (many of you know my relationship with the red bird and my Daddy) visited us. We don't see the red bird that often; you can imagine how we all felt. Then John and Callie had prayer and I was either in a state of "take me Lord" in a good way or "oh yeah, everything will be just fine." From that point on I think John, Callie and LeeAnn will tell you that I went to the hospital so peace-

ful and full of God's grace, it wouldn't have mattered what they were going to do to me.

Then pictures of friends and family in their "Janice Coggins Day" T-shirts started coming over my phone and John, Callie and LeeAnn were outfitted for the hospital in theirs. What an impression they made! My surgeon thought they were the bomb, which they were. I had the best supporters in the hospital, and that is good to know when they come to give you the "night-night" drug.

Back to the family: we have the best family! There is no way I could be where I am today, so strong, without your constant encouragement and love. It is your faith in me, your love for me that I keep in my thoughts as I look down at my LIVESTRONG bracelet. By the way, the LIVESTRONG picture from the beach is AWESOME—Thank you. I can't thank you enough for the role you have played on this journey. We are now on the back nine so stay with me just a little bit longer. Many thanks to Mama's family, as well, for their cards of support. John's family has been equally supportive with calls and cards. So sweet to include me like family as I do them. LeeAnn has been here every day to help me get through this. I couldn't have made it without her. She has truly been an angel.

One thing I know for sure, a cancer diagnosis forces you to look at life more acutely. You don't have to wait for that to happen. Life is now, live life every day, and every day try *to make a difference, and of course apply G.L.U.E.—Give Love Unconditionally Everyday. One last thing, don't put off one thing. Do what you want, or think you need to do, now.*

Love and all of God's blessings,

Jan

P.S. God means for us to be servants. Each of you knows how you have shown up, and I will be forever grateful. I can't ever put into words what my heart feels.

FRIENDS

As I made my journey with cancer, I could *feel* the prayers for me, and I knew—without a doubt—that I was not alone. Cancer was not my friend. But I was *really okay*, because I was packing *so many friends* along with me. Sometimes I would receive a card from a person I had never met. Usually, these cards would come from my mother's or my sister's Sunday school classes. And often, there was a hand-written note as well.

I have chosen to *fully live* my life with ovarian cancer, because I can't do it any other way. I can choose joy over despair, peace over conflict, and happiness over sadness, and—most of the time—I'm glad to say that I make the right choices. That's all I can expect of myself. That, and I try to impact someone else's life in a positive way every day. I can only ask God to bless the many people who have touched and enriched my life, and to give me the strength to return the gesture.

Each of us has received a gift to use to serve others.
—1 Peter 4:10—

ABOUT FAITH: IMPACTING OTHERS

My friend LeeAnn had recently lost her parents. She was standing in line at Starbucks one morning, when the man in front of her turned around and introduced himself. His name was Robb, and he was the executive director of Rx Skin Clinic in Scottsdale, Arizona. LeeAnn had a port wine stain birthmark on her face. And after his introduction, Robb told her that he was an expert in removing birthmarks. He said that he would remove LeeAnn's birthmark in honor of his mother, who had also had them.

LeeAnn was stunned. Her *own* mother had just died only three days before…and now a total stranger told her the story of his own mother, and was offering an amazing gift. When LeeAnn came home, she asked me what I thought about this encounter. I said, "There are no accidents. If you want to get your birthmark removed, then *do* it."

LeeAnn has always maintained that, if you can live through the teasing of grammar school, you don't even think about a birthmark anymore. But she *did* make an appointment to see Robb, and he gave her several treatments. Today, LeeAnn is quite happy with her "new" face. The circumstances of how she met Robb and they made a connection is another good example of how some things may actually be *God's* connection.

When Robb and I met through LeeAnn, I still had my baldhead. It was clear that I was in treatment for cancer. He gave me the warmest hug. And, since he is also bald headed, we laughed together about our heads.

I have since found out that Robb's sister, Jacqui, was diagnosed with Stage Three lung cancer. After he and I made our own connection, he asked if I would mind contacting her to share some of the steps I went through with my own cancer. To this day, Jacqui and I stay in touch. We've shared recipes and books and given each other pep talks. She even participated in a bible study that I conducted even though she lives in Illinois.

It's amazing to think that all this started with Robb and LeeAnn standing in a Starbucks line...or, as Robb likes to say, it started with his Mom having a port wine stain birthmark. It is so ironic how some things play out in life. We just have to be open to allowing God to work in our lives.

ABOUT FAITH: LISTENING

Someone once said most of us die "with the music still in us." I think, how sad that is. When I conduct spiritual retreats, I like to use music. I think it helps set the tone. And we can all use more time to relax and listen.

I once did a retreat for my niece's bible study in Tennessee. I could tell right away that they weren't used to listening to spiritual music. I used several songs that day. As I introduced a new topic, it was interesting to watch who could just *mellow* and allow themselves that *grace space.* God wants our listening time. But it *does* take us *training* our ears to hear Him. You can begin by listening to meaningful music that sends spiritual messages to you.

When I was in the corporate world I would keep a stethoscope on my desk to remind myself to listen. Now, as a trained social worker I'm supposed to be a good listener. But I can tell you, listening is both a *skill* and an *art.* You can become a better listener. But it's important to seek those spaces and places that augment listening… especially to your higher power.

ABOUT FAITH: SYNERGY

When someone gets a cancer diagnosis, they could be tempted to ask the question, "Where is God?" And—when someone gets the news that he or she may have only months to live—"*Where is God?*" really is the question of the hour. These are situations that are enormously difficult. And it's easy to demand that God *fix it.* But I believe that God has a master plan, which we are not meant to know. I also know and believe that God loves us. I do not believe that God sits on a throne and wills *good things* on some people and *bad things* on others. I have heard well-intentioned people say that, "If their faith had been stronger, perhaps the outcome would have been different." I don't believe that, either. I believe some things just *are*.

> *For I know the plans I have for you, declares the Lord,*
> *plans to prosper you and to not harm you,*
> *plans to give you hope and a future.*
> —Jeremiah 29:11—

Many years ago, as a young, inexperienced social worker, I was assigned to the dialysis center at a large medical facility. I met death rather harshly in that job. I found myself asking God many questions…and frankly, getting angry quite often. Finally, I came upon a book written by a rabbi named Harold Kushner, *When Bad Things Happen To Good People*. The book puts in perspective that pain *is* going to happen, people *will* die, natural disasters *will* occur, and all of these events will cause great suffering. But God is not to blame. Rather, God will be there to provide the strength to get us through.

I believe in the power of prayer. And I attribute much of how well I handled my chemotherapy, my surgeries, and all else that my cancer entailed, to the fact that I had so many people praying for me. It is amazing how word of mouth—and now with the advent of the Internet—one can be instantly connected to hundreds of prayer lists and people. That is very powerful. Because, for me, prayer is the medicine that only God can provide. The website, CaringBridge.org is an awesome tool that provides instant sharing with little effort.

According to Drs. Chester L. Tolson, Ph.D. and Harold G. Koenig, M.D. (*The Healing Power Of Prayer*), today many scientists and theologians are realizing that healing is synergistic. Synergism comes from the Greek words *synergia* (meaning "together") and *ergon* (meaning "work"). That is what medicine and prayer must do: they must work *together*.

If prayer has the potential to produce healing, then— just like drugs, surgery, and other therapies—prayer should be ranked with all the other tools humankind has discovered to heal the human body. Prayer heals because it links us with God.

FOCUS

Cancer and cancer treatment are rough yet we have to challenge ourselves to get up every morning, get dressed, show up for the day and have the mind set of not giving cancer the day. There were days when I wasn't my best but I still made a point to show up. I was going to get an "E" for effort no matter what. On those days you may find yourself in what I call a holding pattern, and that's ok. You may not have the energy to make forward progress, sometimes you may regress because the disease becomes too much for a body to endure.

You do have a choice in terms of how you respond to chemo. Some have called for the curtains to be pulled; you can see it in their eyes. Cancer definitely packs that kind of punch and that is a choice for them. There may come a time where I may say I'm done, no more chemotherapy, but for right now I have decided to "buck up" (I think that's a Southern saying), and be a participant in my own rescue.

> *However good or bad a situation is, it will change.*
> *Everyone has their own Mt. Everest to climb.*
> —Hugh Macleod—

FINISH: EYES ON THE PRIZE

For any cancer patient, I think the "prize" has got to be hearing the words, "You are now cancer-free." I know that was cause for my jubilation. I use the words cancer-free but I understand that I have a shadow with me at all times. It is really more semantics, I think, because the term remission was what we used to hear. My thought is, use whatever term feels right for you. Bottom line, I have ovarian cancer and that will not change. At the present time, I do not have an active disease. Just call me NED (no evidence of disease).

But sometimes, when you're in the middle of the fight, it's difficult to keep your "eyes on the prize." So I think it is extremely important to have *goals* that you can look forward to. It doesn't matter what they are. It could be a "cancer-free" life, or an upcoming family reunion…or whatever else inspires you.

In my case, I still had several weeks of chemo left, when my friends Bill and Camille asked if I would like to go with them on a trip to The Holy Land, the following March. This was going to be a pilgrimage leaving from south Louisiana. And, as it turned out, I knew the travel agent who was leading the group. So, after much thought and prayer, I said, "Yes."

For me, a trip to The Holy Land was an amazing *prize* to keep my eyes on. And it turned out to be a life-changer. My faith was strong before I went. But—after walking where Jesus walked—I left Israel affected in a deep and profound way.

I witnessed another "eyes on the prize" moment through LeeAnn. Her parents both were enrolled in hospice, and she was caring for them at home. She asked me if I would help her sister and her at this difficult time in their lives. My primary role was to help LeeAnn stay grounded and help her keep her *eyes on the prize*. In LeeAnn's case, the *prize* was the loving and peaceful presence she could give her parents, supporting them to the end. Even though I had worked with hospice, I had never been close to someone who was losing both parents at the same time. But, by keeping her eyes on the prize, LeeAnn and her sister gave her parents a peaceful and faithful dying process strengthened by God's presence.

MEMORIES

Top: Jan at age 8
Middle: Jan's last day of 18 weeks of chemo with Vicki Aime, chemo nurse, and Beth, "foxhole buddy"
Bottom: Janice's support team on July 12, 2010 just prior to debulking surgery. Nephew John, Niece Callie and LeeAnn

Top: Beth's last day of chemo with Dr. Janicek. I showed up for the celebration.

Middle: Thank you card from Dr. Janicek after being presented with a hand painted special "K". After all, he IS special!

Bottom: Chancellor side of the family stood strong wearing LiveStrong with a wild flare.

Janice after making last mountain pass in Swiss Alps

CHAPTER 5

CANCER "CANS" FOR CAREGIVERS

Cancer *CANS* are thoughts I have about what friends, family and caregivers can do or be for someone with cancer. You can make a difference if you have a loved one diagnosed with cancer by actually *doing* something. Commonly, when someone is trying to help, they'll say, "Call me if you need something." But someone who has just been diagnosed with cancer often doesn't know *what* they need, nor will they be able to articulate it. You, on the other hand, as the person who made the offer need to really think about what you can do

GOODY BAGS

One suggestion is that you CAN just show up with a basket of goodies (i.e. magazines, hand creams, health bars, fresh baked bread, etc.) at your friend's door. Depending on their individual needs, your choice can be varied. Instead of just ordering flowers, I think it's great to personalize your gifts. If flowers are appropriate, make a bouquet of their favorite flowers and deliver them yourself. Or make your gift a *visit,* or a *card*, or *prayers*, or a *meal.*

PHONE CALLS

You CAN also make a personal phone call and check on the patient. The patient will let the call go to voice-mail if she chooses not to answer and will opt to call you back when she is feeling better. However, I would always err on the side of calling rather than wondering, "Oh, I hope Jan is doing okay today." The person going through cancer is overwhelmed; so don't leave it up to them to call you. But if you think a call may be too intrusive, a card, email, or a written note will work equally well.

CHEMO VISITS

Another option is to visit a patient during chemo-therapy. On busy days you may not be able to stay for very long, but it would be a nice surprise and a welcome distraction to have a friend visit. The patient can be on chemo from two to six hours. And a friend is wonderful to have during that treatment time. Our clinic had iPads for us to use, as well. But friends are much better.

CARDS

Cards can be wonderful. I received so many cards in the mail there was not a day that went by that I did not receive something. I have to say that was very humbling.

I also received lots of emails which were very comforting. However, I was usually not up to turning on and sitting at the computer. So, for me, it was nicer to have mail brought to me. I still have my cards that I received, displayed on a tray in my home. Often, I will go by and pull a card out of the stack, read it and enjoy that whole experience all over again. I think cards are very good because they often will come with a handwritten note that really makes a personal connection.

SPECIAL GIFTS

One of my friends in south Louisiana, Dru Patin, made me a silver pendant jewelry necklace, with the letter J. Her note said, "J" is for your name. Or it can be for Jesus, because He's with you." I received so many amazing gifts. One gift Camille sent was a pottery red bird, which now sits on my desk. I look at it every day among other pieces of pottery. I reap the benefits of having a friend who is a master potter.

DONATIONS

You CAN support whichever cancer cause your loved one has, and often you can do something in their honor. That can have a lot of impact. The National Ovarian Cancer Alliance has a remembrance ceremony for celebrating life at their national conference each year whereby they plant seeds in honor of all survivors. You can send a picture and a short note representing that person. I think that's a very neat thing to do. When birthdays, holidays or special days come around and you're not sure what to get that person, you can always donate to their special foundation in their honor. I am sure that will make them very happy.

DINNER ANYONE?

One of the most memorable nights, at the beginning of this cancer journey, was when my friend Jeanie Walsh had me over for dinner in May. The dinner, to my delight, was a full-fledged Thanksgiving dinner for four close friends. She prepared dinner with all the trimmings, because, in her eyes, we truly did have much to be grateful for. This meal was a celebration of gratitude and a pivotal moment for me on this journey. Even though at that time I did have the diagnosis, Jeanie was able to bring us all to see that we still had reason to give thanks. It's in those types of celebrations—which happened throughout my chemotherapy and throughout my treatment—that sustained my grateful attitude. You have probably heard people say, "Cancer is the worst thing that could happen to me." I disagree. It would be far worse for me to lose someone I love in my life, than to have cancer. Jeanie facilitated this gathering and validated my feelings that, even in the face of a storm, you can find reason to give thanks. After all, I am alive!

JUST A VISIT

As Mark Nepo says, "There can be no greater or simpler ambition than to be a friend." Family support was immensely important in my recovery. Yet, because of geographic distance, we often had to be connected via phone or Internet. There is nothing like a personal visit from a friend to cheer you up or a ride to chemo with one of your friends. You can be the friend someone needs to hear from. You can BE THE CONNECTION.

One memorable experience happened after my first surgery. I felt like I'd been hit by an eighteen-wheeler. But suddenly, the doorbell rang, and standing there was a young couple whose wedding I had officiated. They were holding a complete dinner. I went from feeling weak and tired, to peppy and glad. And when they left, I had such a renewed faith in our young people of today and their charity. Taking time out of their busy schedule to visit someone sick and to cook an entire meal, really spoke to their character. I have no doubt Kim and Hector will continue to impact others as they share their compassion and joy.

My friends Bonnie and Steve were similar in their generosity and visits. Bonnie prepared her wonderful lasagna, and we ate that for many meals. It is so helpful to have people that will prepare food for you. When a family is facing cancer, preparing meals is not a priority.

My mind quickly jumps to my friend Kristi's cookies. She baked different varieties such as sugar cookies, peanut butter and molasses. All baked with BUTTER and LOVE, as she knew I needed both. I was trying to increase my appetite and energy, and Kristi knew the trick. Her cookies and her visits were very helpful in my recovery.

PRAY

You CAN continue to pray for a cancer cure. There are many research companies, both small and large, that are working each and every day on finding cures to devastating cancers. In Arizona, we are fortunate to have TGen, the Translational Genomics Research Institute, focused on developing earlier diagnostics and smarter treatments. Thanks to the wonderful scientists that work tirelessly at TGen and other research companies, we now have the knowledge to unravel the genetic components of common and complex diseases.

We also have Dr. Dave Alberts at the University of Arizona in Tucson who helped pioneer new treatments for advanced ovarian cancers. I've personally heard Dr. Alberts on several occasions. His devotion to finding a cure, and his intent on prevention and wellness, makes him one of the most prominent speakers for ovarian cancers in the country. The Susan G. Komen foundation has done a phenomenal job at raising money and awareness for breast cancer. But it's come to the point where we need to spread the word that there are more colors in the rainbow besides *pink*. *Teal* is one of them. We've got to become more of a whole woman and not so part-divided. The Livestrong Foundation addresses cancer in general, which I think is good. Even though he had specific cancer(s), his foundation provides support for people affected by all types of cancer.

CHAPTER 6

KEEPING THE FAITH

Faith is a small word that delivers a lot of punch when we put it into action. When I got diagnosed with cancer, my mind was filled with fear and I needed my faith to get me through this journey. It is then that I picked up my head and said, "I will be faith-based through this ordeal…not fear-based." Of course, there were times when I was fearful, afraid, scared, lonely, and sad. It is healthy and appropriate to have those emotions.

But it is also healthy to stand firm in your faith and to take action with more positive emotions. Bernie Siegel, MD, said, "I have found that four faiths are crucial to recovery from serious illness…faith in one's self, one's doctor, one's treatment and ones spiritual faith."

For me, this journey began with a personal history of strong personal faith. My relationship with God continues to mature with time and life challenges.

I also had tremendous faith in Dr. Janicek…or as I call him, my special "Dr. K." Dr. Janicek is an OBGyn

Oncologist. He knows his field of practice, and exudes confidence. He's a man who loves his work, and it shows.

I also had an equal amount of faith in my chemo nurse, Vicki, and Dr. Janicek's nurse practitioner, Kelly. I have asked each of them how they work with patients whose prognoses isn't always positive. Kelly answered, "There's always the element of sadness…and a little bit of us goes away every time we lose a patient. But I consider it a blessing to work with you and get to know you."

Vicki told me that sometimes she wrestles with her job, and there are days that she thinks about quitting because emotionally it's so difficult. But then she'll receive a thank-you note from a patient. And that will be *just* what she needs. She said that when a patient dies, she always takes an emotional hit. But then she'll meet another incredibly feisty woman in the office who is ready to kick cancer to the curb.

Dr. Janicek and his staff have a difficult job meeting the needs of their patients. As a patient, I like to think that we do something for them. I like to think that, at the end of the day, I've given them some joy. Being joyful can be a "cancer buster." Use it frequently.

CHAPTER 7

SHARING THE JOY

I was heading to work at the golf shop one day, when I saw two couples in the breezeway taking pictures. I offered to take a picture of the four of them. While we were shooting, one of the gentlemen told me he liked my short hair. "Well, thank you," I said. "It's just coming back after cancer treatment." The other gentleman looked at me and said, "I am a survivor as well." At that point, we all started whooping and hollering and high-fiving. Then the first gentleman said he had something to give me. He reached into his pocket and pulled out four small rocks. Anybody who knows me, knows that I love rocks. Rocks and stones are just special to me. "All of these rocks have been blessed," the man told me. So, I picked out a rock for myself. And the man looked me in the eyes and said, "You have a blessed day." Then, they all walked away.

So, there I stood, with this neat little rock, thinking *what just happened?* To me, this is another story of how staying *open to the moment* allows us to bring joy to each other and impact others.

Here are some ideas for a joy-full day:

- Give thanks throughout the day.
- Laugh often.
- Appreciate the small and large things that come your way.
- See love all around you.
- Look for the sun and to the Son.
- Spread your wings.
- Do something out of the ordinary.
- Be creative.
- Take deep breaths.
- Smile, and then smile some more.
- Sing while you are driving.
- Make peace your soul mate.
- Have momentary miracles often, and then share them with others.
- Greet everyday like it's your last.
- Embrace the sacred.
- Live in the NOW.

UNTIL FURTHER NOTICE, CELEBRATE EVERYTHING

During your cancer treatment, it is quite possible to feel like a "normal" person. Great strides have been made in complementary drugs that are given, along with the cancer drugs, resulting in feelings of normalcy. This is not to say that side effects do not exist. But for the most part, they can be managed.

When you're having a good day, take advantage of celebrating by doing something that makes you feel good. Some examples may be just sitting in your back yard getting some Vitamin D, or reading a book on your front porch. Perhaps you could have a lunch date with a good friend or a massage. I have a massage therapist, Kim, who isn't just a massage therapist. She is like my other team members. She really cares about my well being. I would suggest that one seek a practitioner using that as a guide.

Cancer gives us the gift of knowing, at a gut level, what feels good to us. My friend, Beth, gets a pedicure often and always gets a teal color on her toes. Whatever gift you give yourself will be the right one.

CHAPTER 8

THE JOURNEY CONTINUES

I believe there is an art to living. I think there is no problem presented to us, without a purpose for making us stronger. Frederich Neitzsche, a German philosopher, said, "That which does not kill us makes us stronger." For me, living is in the giving and not in the getting. If we can remember that in our daily lives, much angst could be lifted. Speaking for myself, having a heart of gratitude for what I have far exceeds sitting around wishing things were different.

Sometimes a cancer diagnosis can cause us to panic, and we perceive that it is too much for us to handle. But if you can *lean into the cancer,* you can find your courage and inner strength. For me, my faith has always been solid. But I probably have never *leaned into it* quite like I did on this journey with cancer. By *leaning into it,* I mean I let it help support me through prayer, talking to others about my faith, reading my bible, and other inspirational materials. This may not be for everyone. I'm a proponent for people finding comfort in their own skin. And I think it is really healthy for every individual to find what works for him or her. But for me, my faith was comforting.

It was also important for me to speak freely about my cancer. Once I was bald, it was easier to address it. I found that talking about it helped put people at ease. And each time I told my story, and I looked into someone else's eyes, and I made a connection, I got strength. I believe in the human connection and its powerful effect on one's mental and spiritual being.

We are not human beings having a spiritual existence.
We are spiritual beings having a human existence.
—Teilhard de Chardin—

When we're going through our cancer treatments, it stirs compassion in others. This may be our psyche's way of protecting us. But, personally, I believe when we allow ourselves to feel true compassion for each other, we have opened up the opportunity for joy as well.

During our grief-filled moments we need to be reminded that there is opportunity for grace. God is always near. I have never felt closer to God than with my experience with cancer.

God was ever-present in my life. Like a child with her blanket, I had God, I wore God, I talked God, I prayed God. He was and is my Source.

There's a bracelet that my friend Beth gave me that I love. On it is written all the things that cancer can**not** do. Cancer can**not** rob you of your soul. Your soul is sacred, God made you in his likeness and he sees you as beautiful. Cancer can**not** steal eternal life, or conquer the spirit, or cripple love, or kill friendship, or suppress memories, or corrode faith, or shutter hope, or destroy peace, or silence courage, or invade the soul.

What lies behind us and what lies before us are
small matters compared to what lies within us.
—Ralph Waldo Emerson—

In his book, *The Book of Awakening,* Mark Nepo suggests that we must learn to "marry one's soul." The *nautical* definition of "marry" is to join two ropes end-to-end by interweaving their strands. "To marry one's soul suggests that we interweave the life of one spirit with the life of our psychology. The life of our heart with the life of our mind, the life of our faith and truth with the life of our doubt and anxiety. And, just as two ropes that are married create a tie that is twice as strong, when we marry our humanness to our spirit we create a life that is doubly strong in the world."

Cancer has no place in our soul and spirit. It may invade our bodies but we can decide to let *that* be the boundary. Our spirit can continue to give energy and love. We can embrace all that is good and pure; we can take deep breaths, watch sunsets and give thanks even in the face of cancer. This is what spirit-filled people do to take care of their souls. Remember, your soul wasn't surgically cut. You are whole. And you are holy.

EPILOGUE

As I had learned, late stage ovarian cancer has a high rate of recurrence. In December 2012, my own cancer had returned. Even though I was very aware of the statistics—I had been healthy for two years—this news knocked me completely off center once again.

After taking some time to absorb the reality, I am happy to be able to say that I am once again applying the five important anchors (family, friends, faith, focus, finish) that so helped me through my first battle with this disease. My attitude remains positive, and I continue to have great faith in my doctor and my healthcare team. But the recurrence has taught me, there is one final "F" that may be the most important of all…FIGHTER.

GRACE SPACE

A LOOK INTO MY PERSONAL JOURNAL

During my cancer journey, which I call my Grace Space, writing in my journal allowed me to make sense of my thoughts during this difficult time in my life... helped me clear my head, make sense of my emotions and find a stronger path to walk with God. Below are some excerpts from my Grace Space journal, exactly as I wrote them (flaws and all) during my journey through cancer.

MAY 10, 2010:

My journal will be turned sideways from now on since my life has been turned a few degrees on its side. Two weeks ago, I learned I have dual cancers, actually a tumor taking space in my uterus, ovaries and abdominal wall. I now have had my first chemo treatment and will have eight more before surgically removing the tumor. I was caught blind-sided by the cancer diagnosis and all that it entails.

LeeAnn has been such a trooper, in fact she was the one who told me that I have cancer. I think in some ways it has been just as hard on her. We both have reached out to God and each other and it's been calming. In a strange way like the calm you get before the storm. They say the center of the storm is the calmest, well maybe we're trying our best to stay in that center. The storm does hit you throughout the day and when you feel sick and don't want to eat, tired, can't sleep and you know you have a monster living in you. The storm hits, but the trick is to not let it linger long.

Pretend God's breath is brushing everything away from you, through you, and receive His blessings and his healing. No doubt it is a challenge but my inner strengths of determination and faith will see me through. I don't know what my future holds but I know who my future is with and that's enough for me right now. My family has been awesome through this, I know it's been tough on them but I would rather it be me than any of them. I think of my father often. He died March 31, 2009. It has only been a little over a year and I miss his presence, especially during this time.

My friends have been off the charts, I didn't know I had so many. Camille is flying out here today to stay four days. Camille and I worked together at the University in Louisiana and at Lafayette General Medical Center. We have been friends for a long time.

John and Callie were here before I was hardly out of surgery. I will hold that so dear because I can say, "I have loved those two children probably more than the law allows," a southern expression my Dad would say. They're the children I never had. God blessed me with such wonderful relationships with each of them.

I am grateful for all of my family. Their faith has touched me profoundly. I know I am the one going through cancer and I am not bitter that it is me. I can't explain that. I'm not happy about it, I don't want cancer but of the children in my family, I would rather it be me.

The plan I was facing included 18 total weeks of chemotherapy and surgery in this order: nine weeks with chemotherapy, three weeks off for de-bulking surgery and 9 more weeks of chemo to attack microscopic cells after surgery. So I was looking at 4-5 months of treatment and I wanted to make the house more comfortable for me. I knew I would be spending more time around the house, so I might as well make the changes that would make me comfortable. The first thing I did was I put up eight family collage pictures. My family is in Colorado, Tennessee and Mississippi; I needed them close to me. My friends are also spread out throughout the country, so going through pictures and hanging them in the hallway was fun.

I got my sanctuary in order, which is the room in our home where I read, pray, write and enjoy just hanging out. I also knew we may be having more overnight company, therefore, I decided to add a futon. About the futon; my wonderful friends Suzanne and Gail came up to visit from Tucson several times throughout my chemotherapy. Suzanne is the premiere shopper, I had no idea where to look for a futon but somehow Suzanne knew about a futon store. So off we go to buy a futon that works beautifully in my sanctuary. It's been a great addition, especially for my naps.

During this process I felt like I was a pregnant woman getting ready for a baby. It was just so interesting to watch how intent I was on getting the house in order. Who knows if all of what I did really helped me, I personally think it did and that's all that matters. I think each person will know what they will need to do to ready them for something they've never had to combat. For me my home is sacred space and my refuge. I knew I needed that to be as comfortable as possible because I was going out into a "cancer war zone."

Chemotherapy isn't to be taken lightly. It conquers all cells, both good and bad. I chose to focus on what it would do to eradicate my cancer. It may be semantics but it starts with how one believes in their therapy and stays focused on the GOOD in the approach.

I had a particular way I dressed for chemo, a look if you will. It was a comfortable upbeat look, such as bright orange shoes, that worked for me. My shoes were cool Keen sandals and I wore my comfortable jeans with a favorite T-shirt. I wanted to be comfortable and relaxed at each treatment. I was going to be the brightest light in the room. I believed I had to fight with all the gusto I could drum up, because I knew the chemo drugs weren't necessarily going to be great and wonderful. I also made a point to go to lunch after each treatment with the friend who drove me. It was a celebration and I would insist on treating. We would have a blast.

Vicki, the chemo nurse would also send us off after each treatment with a hug. And, if Paola was around, she would do the same. And of course, Dr. Janicek gives the best hugs. The point here is you have to do what you can to keep your spirits high, have an attitude of gratitude and be open to NOW moments. That's when we can win. Cancer can't take our spirits when we're living in the now. It's when we give cancer our future, then I think of Russian Roulette, and I don't like that game. Now is the only time we have.

I will be okay.

The way I've lived my life has allowed me to be probably more ready to withstand what is before me. The hospice patients that I worked with in the past few decades gave me the greatest gift by opening my eyes to the fact that we only have NOW. I did much in my earlier life and saw so much and experienced God through the eyes of people who knew what it was like to live like you were dying, which is the way we all should live.

"I can be better or bitter; I choose to be better."

Cancer allows you to become very acute to everything around. Tim McGraw's song "Live Like You Were Dying" should be everyone's song, not just people with cancer or a terminal illness. I've always liked that song and received a

card from someone I hardly knew that reminded me of it.
It's been great to listen to it again, and yes that's how we are
supposed to live. My hospice patients taught me that a long
time ago; don't put off, live now, God is NOW.

I cannot change the past and the future is uncertain. We
just know God's in the NOW and that's good enough for
me. Since my diagnosis friends have called, visited, emailed,
skyped, mailed cards, etc. which has been amazing and powerful. Even connections with people I didn't really know have
been extremely impacting. One example is Patti, my nutritionist, who is a friend of Bonnie's. She has ended up being
like an angel and connected with me on a soul level. I am
reminded daily of how blessed I am.

MAY 20, 2010:

Another day after chemo; feeling well, chemo went well.
I met an amazing woman who was having her last chemo
appointment yesterday, her name was Rhonda and she was
filled with joy and I really liked her. She gave me the name
of her acupuncturist and she also suggested a book for me
to read, The Anticancer New Way of Life Book by David
Servan-Schreiber, M.D., Ph.D. This is also the book that
Patti, my nutritionist, suggested that I read. I was really im-
pressed with Rhonda and how she had handled her chemo,
and we promised to stay in touch with each other.

During our last meeting the other day, Patti challenged
me to think about who I will become after cancer treatment.

I was puzzled by her question but I've begun to think about that. I think I'm already getting a glimpse. It's all about being in the now and being present and it's not so much about doing. I'm still doing things but definitely at a different pace; there's not so much a sense of urgency.

Being real is very important, and definitely the moment to moment living is your focus. I think cancer patients are very much given the gift of life, even though it's somewhat of a different position. When people think about getting a cancer diagnosis, they often think of death, when, in reality, they are given life. We're all just a breath away from death, it's just that people don't stop and think about that. No one knows when they're going to die. It's important that we all live everyday as if it were our last. If we did that, we would all be kinder, gentler, more patient, more loving and more full of life.

"The will of God will never take you where the grace of God will not protect you" (unknown.) Church Sunday was the Feast of Pentecost, it was my first time to attend service since my diagnosis. I experienced so many emotions. I was so glad to be in church and that we were celebrating the Holy Spirit.

JUNE 14, 2010:

Long time since I last wrote in my journal. This was my sister Suzie's second visit. We so enjoyed her. She was very present, we went shopping and she insisted on buying me a pair of loop earrings, the silver ones that I wear now, since I now have a bald head. Losing my hair was just another one of those cancer zaps. Just last week Rhonda and I were having lunch and a man came up to our table to tell me that I looked like his daughters. He was having lunch with his foursome from golf. He shared the story that both of his daughters had cancer, were bald and both daughters were going through breast cancer. Rhonda and I were both brought to tears because his story was so touching and he was so kind. When the waitress came around to get our order we had to waive her off, as we were still thinking of this stranger sharing the intimacy of his life with us. It was powerful.

I felt like after he left our table that I really had been touched by an angel. I also think, my bald head invited him to share that story with us and make an unexpected connection that day. We all smiled following our conversation.

JUNE 15, 2010:

Thought for the day: remain porous. Getting a cancer diagnosis hits you like a brick wall, literally. So the trick is to allow yourself to hit the brick wall and then open yourself up, meaning open your heart, your head, your arms; let everything run through and do not allow anything to attach itself to you. Just be porous, be open. When you hit the brick wall you have been stopped in your tracks and now must do your best to embrace it and make the most of it. There will always be that shadow looming; it's the elephant in the room that wasn't there before. One's life totally hinges on CA 125 count from this point on. It changes your life.

Psalms 23, The Lord is My Shepherd I Shall Not Want, has been a constant meditation for me. It's just one that is very calming and I often say that when I become anxious, because there is no doubt there are a lot of unknowns even though you may know your diagnosis and what's in store for you. There's always the every-three-month-testing. This is an anxiety producing event. No doubt about it.

This is a different version of Psalms 23: (I like it)

The Lord is my constant companion. There is no need He cannot fulfill. Whether His course for me points to the mountaintops of glorious ecstasy or the valleys of human suffering, He is by my side, He is ever present with me. He is close beside me when I tread the dark streets of danger, and even when I flirt with death itself, He will not leave me. When the pain is severe, He is near to comfort. When the burden is heavy, He is there to lean upon. When depression darkens my soul, He touches me with eternal joy. When I feel empty and alone, He fills the aching vacuum with his power. My security is in his promise to be near to me always, and in the knowledge that He will never let me go. (by Leslie Brandt, from the book "Psalms Now.")

JUNE 22, 2010:

This past week I felt like a cancer patient. I had diarrhea for a week and current medications are not working, so I called my chemo nurse Vicki and she called in something stronger. It just wasn't a lot of fun being sick that way. I knew I had cancer in previous weeks, but now with unrelieved side effects, like diarrhea, I now feel that cancer has me. I thought I was in control of cancer. WRONG.

The head game is to tell yourself, "This is not going to beat me. Use my resources and get help today to stay in the game and fight this beast." Staying in the game is the key, believe in the treatment that you chose and believe in the people that are caring for you. Stay focused.

This week I told our pool man Joe that I had cancer. He is the nicest man and he loves my dog Hudson. He is always giving him treats. He and his wife sent me a card that they were praying for me during treatment. I cried when I received their card; it really touched me.

Yesterday was Callie's birthday, we can't celebrate enough how precious she is to all of us. I hope she knows that I ask God to continue to bless and protect her. I continue to live with a grateful heart.

JUNE 29, 2010:

My sister Suzie was here this weekend, we had a great visit and she continues to be very encouraging and supportive.

I could feel it. We laughed a lot and I also had my first yoga class which Suzie got to attend with me. Yoga class was great, 13 ladies, all about my age and one even had a bald head. She had breast cancer and finished her chemo in April.

My upcoming surgery (to remove the cancer tumor and total hysterectomy) is scheduled for July 12th. The thought of another surgery is causing some pause, looking forward to it most of the time. No one likes to think about a big surgery but we're all called to surrender. I must and I will call upon my faith. I will pray for strength and courage. I am not too worried about the recovery. I heal well and I'll have plenty of people to help me. Sometimes I am in disbelief that I have cancer, it's happened so quickly and I've just started treatments. From time to time you do ask yourself is this really happening? And of course the answer is, yes it is. That's when you have to really focus on the moment, your breath, because your breath is life and trust that if **GOD LEADS YOU TO IT, HE WILL LEAD YOU THROUGH IT.**

One thing I have noticed through this is that I have had more patience and God given grace. I've have been more humbled by this experience than anything I have ever experienced. Actually I am experiencing exactly what I observed when I was working with hospice. I would see people in their late 50's early 60's retire, just at the age when they were getting ready to travel and do all the things that they had been waiting to do and yet they got a cancer diagnosis. Yet I was fortunate enough back in my 30's when I was working with hospice and saw that happen time and time again.

One day, I decided to do something about it. I wanted to move through life without regrets and to start at that moment. I took off for a year and traveled all over the world. I owe my hospice patients a big thank you for giving me that gift of how life is so eminent, it is now.

Don't wait for a cancer diagnosis to get that. The essence of my life hasn't changed because of my cancer diagnosis but certainly the conditions have. I will continue to live each day like I've hopefully lived every day of my life and that's with a grateful heart and with what I like to call G.L.U.E., which stands for Giving Love Unconditionally Everyday, and try to make a difference in someone else's life.

It's probably better not to focus as much on the fact that we have cancer but rather how we are being changed by it. Just as life is not about what we have or what we are able to purchase, but it is about what we BECOME as human beings, and that is an ever changing process. Which is why I give cancer some credit. I am a better person because of my cancer.

I am much more patient with myself and others. There is not a moment that goes by that I am not grateful. Cancer survivors get a double dose of knowing how to live in the moment. *You hear people speak of that often but people who have had their number called, really understand that life is fragile and can be snuffed out way too soon.*

JULY 22, 2010:

Today is my 59th birthday and I am sharing it with my sister and brother-in-law, John. My sister and I have not been together for a birthday since we were kids. They arrived from Tennessee with the car loaded with fresh vegetables and other delectable foods. John immediately made homemade soup and Jeannette prepared breakfast each day.

I was not eating well, post-operative, but somehow their food increased my appetite, making food appealing. Jeannette baked a fresh apple cake for my birthday. My family has been a pillar of strength and my older sister has taken over the kitchen, thank goodness, and can give Paula Dean a run for her money. Each day I am getting stronger and stronger. John is doing his part by entertaining me with his war stories. By the time they left (two weeks), I was ready for the next round of chemo. I had truly been spoiled by southern comfort. We were left with loads of food in the freezer and wonderful memories and received healing at a base level.

JULY 31, 2010:

Camille and Sister Doris came to visit me for a week. I was 3 weeks post-op from the big surgery, still recovering to get my strength back and getting ready for the next round of chemotherapy. Their visit included food from South Louisiana, like homemade pralines (Sister Doris's specialty), crawfish etoufee, fresh okra, homemade granola bars. It was a great time to have friends around as I recuperated. It was comforting and full of laughter that serves to heal your soul.

Camille, Sister Doris and I had worked together at Lafayette General Medical Center so we had many mutual friends/colleagues. Sister Doris still works at Lafayette General as a chaplain and worked with another colleague, Cindy Angelle, to take pictures of my friends back home. She brought over 50 pictures with messages for me and we went through them over and over. I had left Lafayette and LGMC in 1997 so not all the names came to mind immediately (maybe it was chemo), but the faces and smiles brought joy and happiness.

SIGNS, STATISTICS AND RISK FACTORS

SYMPTOMS OF OVARIAN CANCER

Beware of the following changes in your body:

- Bloating
- Pelvic and abdominal pain
- Difficulty eating or feeling full quickly
- Urinary symptoms (urgency or frequency)
- Fatigue
- Indigestion
- Back pain
- Pain with intercourse
- Constipation
- Menstrual irregularities
- Unexplained weight loss or gain
- Shortness of breath

OVARIAN CANCER STATISTICS

Ovarian cancer strikes many women each year. As of January 2008, there were 177,578 women alive in the

United States that had been diagnosed with Ovarian Cancer (CDC publication #99-99124 "Get the Facts About Gynecological Cancer, May 2010"). The projected incidence for ovarian cancer in 2011 was 21,990 with 15,460 projected deaths. Though ovarian cancer accounts for three percent of cancers in women, it is the fifth leading cause of cancer death among women and the deadliest of gynecological cancers.

RISK FACTORS FOR OVARIAN CANCER

Check for risk factors for ovarian cancer:

- Inherited genetic mutations often exhibited in family or
  personal history of breast, colon rectal or ovarian cancer
- Family history of ovarian cancer
- Personal history of cancer
- Age
- Reproductive history and infertility
- Hormone Replacement Therapy
- Obesity

CANCER CANS

When someone near or dear to you has cancer:

- You can make a difference.
- You can call and check on the patient.

- You can visit them at chemotherapy, if this is an option.
- You can send cards, emails or texts.
- You can continue to pray for cancer cures.

REFERENCES

- Several translations of the Bible were used.
- Brandt, Leslie, *Psalms Now.* St. Louis, MO: Concordia Publishing House, 1973.
- *Get to Know the Facts on Ovarian Cancer* (2010, CDC Publication).
- Kushner, Harold, *When Bad Things Happen To Good People.* New York, NY: Random House, 1978.
- Nepo, Mark, *The Book of Awakening.* York Beach, ME: Conari Press, 2000
- Dr. Chester L. Tolson and Dr. Harold G. Koenig, *The Healing Power of Prayer.* Grand Rapids, MI: Baker Books, 2003.
- Dr. Jill Bolt Taylor, *My Stroke of Insight.* New York, NY: Viking, 2008.
- Servan- Schriebier, David, *The Anticancer: The New Way Life.* New York, NY: Viking, 2008.
- Siegel, Bernie, *Love, Medicine, Miracles.* New York, NY: Harper Collins Publishing, 1986.

CPSIA information can be obtained
at www.ICGtesting.com
Printed in the USA
BVOW06s2131230817
492961BV00009B/93/P